Wilderness Generation

Lance Ainsworth

Lance Ainsworth Ministries

PastorLAinsworth@gmail.com

www.LanceAinsworth.com

ISBN-13: 978-0692945452
ISBN-10: 0692945458

I dedicate this to my amazing wife Olivia, who has stood by my side and always believed and encouraged me to follow God's call on my life.

Table of Contents

FOREWORD

Reading the *Wilderness Generation* highlighted the importance of my spiritual heritage in my mind. My great-grandfather on my Dad's side of the family was a fill-in itinerant preacher in the Presbyterian denomination. My grandfather on my Mom's side was a Baptist deacon who deeply loved the Church and felt called of God to stand beside and behind his Pastor in every way. I have been told stories of how he would bounce me on his knee and pray that I would serve God all the days of my life. I have been a follower of Christ for forty-one years. I have been speaking and preaching the Gospel for forty years and I expect to have many more fruitful years of ministry. My reason for delving into my spiritual heritage while writing this foreword is due to the fact that I have always declared over my children that in Jesus' name they would, "Go farther, higher, deeper and do greater things than me," which is now happening.

In reading this book that Lance has written I have realized that he has captured the heart of his generation and expressed it in written form in a way that I never could. For most of my life I have been preaching and speaking to his generation, but now it seems as though he is standing on my shoulders peering over the fence viewing the future from a perspective that only keen insight and the Holy Spirit could give.

If you are a parent, teacher, Pastor, or you just have a desire to reach MILLENNIALS for the cause of Christ and His Kingdom then you must read and heed the counsel of this book.

Immediately after finishing the book I felt an incredible desire to do something to reach the eighty-three million MILLENNIALS in America. I even crafted a two week mini-series called "What Would Jesus Say to MILLENNIALS?" I preached it to the church that I currently pastor. The response to it was amazing because I used some of the strategies and information found within the *Wilderness Generation*. Therefore, I believe that Generations Church now has a revelation and motivation to reach out to MILLENNIALS.

WARNING: READ WITH CAUTION, YOU MAY BE MOVED TO EXTREME ACTION AS A RESULT OF FINISHING THIS BOOK!

Ed Ainsworth

INTRODUCTION

Millennials! There are stacks of books, numerous TED Talks, seminars, publications, blogs, vlogs, conferences, and even sermons that try to unlock the mystery of the millennial generation. So why should you read this book? What makes this one so different from other resources? In America and around the world, there is a growing interest in the millennial generation. Focus groups, families, communities and corporations are starting to notice stark differences between generation X, baby boomers, and millennials.

Some people label millennials as lazy, entitled, narcissistic, materialistic, dreamers, and privileged. Others empathize with this generation by acknowledging their ideologies and philosophies of life. One thing all of us can agree on is – this generation, *my* generation, is unique. There has never been one like it before.

The millennial generation was born during 1982-2000 and number 83.1 million in America. This is one-quarter of our nation's population; more than baby boomers and more than African Americans and Asian Americans combined. Millennials are the most educated generation in our history, with 34 percent achieving a bachelor's degree. Millennials are entrepreneurs. They have started more than double the number of businesses of any generation. Millennials are tech-savvy, cause-driven, progressive, and team-oriented, and I believe the Lord wants to use the millennial generation to see the promise of God fulfilled.

During a critical transition in my life, the Lord spoke explicitly to me and revealed that I am a Joshua. At that moment, I had no idea what He meant or where that word would take me. At the time, I was hired to run a Bible school where students ranged from ages 18–32. I was thankful for the opportunity, but realized I was in over my head so I sought God asking, "What kind of a leader do you want me to be? What's my leadership style? What's my role in this season?" With absolute certainty, the Lord replied, "You are a Joshua. I have ordained you to lead people out of the wilderness and into the promise of God." To this day, I am learning and seeking out the depth of this call.

As I began to research Joshua and the wilderness generation, I noticed some distinct similarities between Israel's Old and New Testament generations and the millennial generation of today. I believe there are conclusive parallels between the two generations and that's what separates this book from other resources. The Word of God has been given to us as a guide for our present and future. In God's Word, we can find the answer to every problem we face. I believe the Bible answers the questions we are asking about the millennial generation. The focus of this book is to explore biblical truths and their relevance for us today.

The wilderness was a place of testing, trials, self-discovery, and ultimately, perfection. Many great men were called into the wilderness for a season; David, Elijah, John the Baptist, and the Lord Himself, Jesus Christ who braved the wilderness 40 days. The number 40 is mentioned 146 times throughout scripture and symbolizes a period of testing and trials. The children of Israel wandered in the wilderness 40 years on a journey that had the potential of taking merely 11 days. We embrace the season of the wilderness, but we don't find comfort in it. God never meant for us to wander in isolation, but He will use isolation to perfect us for the promise.

The conundrum of millennials is that they are leaving the church and religion in general. They have no desire to keep things status quo and the church has not been able to explain why this is happening or formulate a solution. My prayer is that this book will present great insight to both the millennials and those who desire to see millennials reach their potential in Christ. Though I will speak in some generalities, I understand I can never stereotype or judge every person from every generation. God has always raised up men and women who don't fit the mold of culture around them, and my purpose is not to limit any individual by the consensus of the majority. In fact, if you feel like you don't identify with those around you and the pitfalls of this generation, then you will be even more encouraged as you read and realize God has called you to be a Joshua to lead your peers into the *promised land.*

The eye-opening similarities between millennials and the *wilderness generation of today* – the *Joshua wilderness generation,* may surprise you. Whether you are a millennial or someone who intends to better understand millennials, this journey is going to enlighten, clarify, rebuke and inspire you. I have laid out the roadmap in this order: The Shift, Preparing for Promotion, The Call to Joshua, and The Promise. So let's begin!

THE TRANSFORMATION

Transformation: change in form, nature or character. In this context, we are not talking about a physical transformation, but a heart one. In thinking through the concepts of this book, I believe the Lord led me to write about four core seasons of the wilderness generation who followed Joshua. The first season is *The Transformation.*

As we pick up the story in Joshua 1, God assigned Joshua the new leader of the children of Israel and there was a mandate on his life to renew the people's mindset. Joshua witnessed firsthand the disposition of the people; the bickering, complaining, the stiff-necked attitude. He was exasperated. He knew that for Israel to see God's promise, there had to be an attitude check. Like my father always says, "You better check yourself before you wreck yourself."

I believe God calls us to *do something* about issues that grieve us; circumstances we just can't tolerate and hope to change. In this case, Joshua was grieved about the unfulfilled promise of God. He knew for the promise to come to pass, there had to be a change.

What are the things in our culture or society you cannot overlook? What gets under your skin? I know my wife's pet peeve is disingenuous people, so she is called to foster genuine relationships and cultivate life-giving communities rather than superfluous meetings. I can't accept lethargic, wandering, purposeless living, so God called me to motivate people into their God-given purpose. I believe we all need a heart transformation if we are going to make the difference in our world God is drawing us into.

This transformation comes in three stages. First, we must believe God is a contemporary God and that He still desires to move miraculously through signs and wonders. Second, we must consecrate ourselves to declare ourselves as God's. Third, we must pursue new provision. With new vision comes new provision.

WITH NEW VISION COMES NEW PROVISION.

Throughout these early chapters, I ask that you open your heart to God. Whether you have been a Christian your entire life or don't even identify with being a Christian, I know the Lord wants to speak to you. He wants to revolutionize your perspective about His feelings for you and our generation. Invite Him to transform your mindsets and attitudes.

Chapter 1

A CONTEMPORARY GOD

"…as I was with Moses, *so* I will be with you." (Joshua 1:5 NKJV)

Is God still relevant? Does He still move? Does He understand the current cultural climate and if so, then what is His role? Countless people wandering in the wilderness are asking similar questions. They're familiar with Christianity. They know about Jesus and they believe there is a God, but their bigger question is, "So how does knowing God make me different than anybody else?" Joshua is our example of triumph in the wilderness. He reached the Promised Land despite overwhelming obstacles. Joshua 1:5 reminds us – Joshua needed reassurance that God was still with him just as He was with his predecessor, Moses. He essentially petitioned God, "Are You still with us and do You still have a purpose for us now?"

One day our church elder, Charles Curle shared some valuable God-given insight. Charles is a man I deeply respect. He has an amazing legacy and when he speaks, I listen. His children serve the Lord, his grandchildren serve the Lord, and they all do it with much joy and deep devotion. He is the inspiration behind the name of this chapter. He said, "Lance, God is a contemporary God. He is relevant, and he will never stop being relevant. We will never lose our need for God." Charles explained that God does not grow old. He is not an idea we outgrow. God knows how to reach each generation on their level. God is still a contemporary God. He is still speaking and He is still reaching out to us. He is still pursuing. He still loves us despite the weakness of our fleshly character.

> GOD IS A CONTEMPORARY GOD. HE IS RELEVANT, AND HE WILL NEVER STOP BEING RELEVANT. WE WILL NEVER LOSE OUR NEED FOR GOD.
> -CHARLES CURLE

The definition of *contemporary* is to belong or occur in the present. Our God occurs in the present.

Deuteronomy 34 chronicles the death of Moses. Moses the savior, Moses the hero, Moses the father, Moses the deliverer, and Moses the connection to God... was gone! A generation was faced with a choice. “Was this faith just for my forefathers or is it also for me?” It’s a choice every generation must confront when stepping into its own belief system.

Some would say it was a no-brainer, but this is a wilderness generation we’re talking about. It had been wandering 40 years with no land to call its own. Each person endured the whining, complaining and murmuring of his elders about this God who left them to die.

And the children of Israel said to Moses, "Oh, that we had died by the hand of the Lord in the land of Egypt, when we sat by the pots of meat and when we ate bread to the full! For you have brought us out into this wilderness to kill this whole assembly with hunger." (Exodus 16:3 NKJV)

The Joshua generation, the wilderness generation, watched their parents surrender everything to follow God and yet they still had not received the promise. Would they stand on the principles of their fathers or discard the lineage of faith?

How many times have we painfully watched a generation stop believing in God because the children carry the hurt of their parents? They say things like, "My mom asked to be healed of cancer, but she died." Or, "My grandparents went to church every time the doors were open and they were no different from anyone else."

Religious ties and denominational rituals are beginning to blur into the past. Millennials see less and less importance in rituals as we develop a clearer focus of the realities of life. Our generation desires to see religion become more relevant to help us navigate social injustice, the purpose of mankind, secular humanism, racial reconciliation, and world hunger, just to name a few. We ask, "What good are your rituals to me if they don't change my current realities or the world?"

Like the wilderness generation of the Bible, our generation is disconnected by empty religion that focuses on works. We want to see true change, not just a feeling one might get in a church service, but instead – a *movement.* Our God is not a God of dos and don'ts rather, He has written a love story devoted to His love for mankind.

Reflecting on history, it appeared religion and religious organizations placed the emphasis on what mankind built in the past, so much so, that we have lost sight of *what is* – the reality right in front of us. We serve a contemporary God. *Everything that once was is now climaxing into what is.*

The millennial generation, the wilderness generation of today, perceive God and religion as a part of our culture for only a time. They regard religious traditions as something our parents practiced and something used to manipulate people. When you really think about the history of the world, men have many times used the Word of God as a manipulative ploy to minimize a group of people. We don't always associate God and church in a positive light. I believe our generation is faced with a Peter moment.

Jesus asked His disciples, Who do men say that I, the Son of Man, am?

So they said, Some say John the Baptist, some Elijah, and others Jeremiah or one of the prophets. He said to them, But who do you say that I am? Simon Peter answered and said, You are the Christ, the Son of the living God. Jesus answered and said to him, Blessed are you, Simon Bar-Jonah, for flesh and blood has not revealed this to you, but My Father who is in heaven. And I also say to you that you are Peter, and on this rock I will build My church, and the gates of Hades shall not prevail against it. And I will give you the keys of the kingdom of heaven, and whatever you bind on earth will be bound in heaven, and whatever you loose on earth will be loosed in heaven." (Matthew 16:13-20 NKJV)

I just love how Jesus set this up. It speaks volumes. He began with asking, "How does the world see me?" Then He asked, "How do you view me?" It's as if He's saying, "It doesn't matter what others *think*, it matters what you *know*." Peter's answer was right on. Jesus is the Son of the living God, and He is the answer. He is the One we have been waiting for and He is the One who changes everything. He is the Promised One.

Jesus is asking us if we know who He is. Do we have a true revelation of Him? Once we get a revelation, He will build His church. The church is built upon the revelation of Jesus and He will do great things on that foundation. Then in verse 19, He says He will give us the keys to the Kingdom and we will have authority from Heaven. Just as God is contemporary, He will

THE CHURCH IS BUILT UPON THE REVELATION OF JESUS.

make us contemporary. He will make us relevant to the present. It doesn't matter what the world's view is of Jesus. He just needs a few people to get a truthful revelation of who He is.

Through the ages, self-righteous, power hungry, egotistical, and self-centered people have dared to use the Bible to confirm their evil desires, and yet God has kept His Word alive for such a time as this. When authentic, honest, loving people come to know Jesus as Lord, He says to them what God said to Joshua, "As I was with Moses, so I will be with you. I will not leave you nor forsake you." (Joshua 1:5 NKJV)

This is so important because of what God was to Moses. He was the "I am" to Moses. "And God said to Moses, "I AM WHO I AM."" (Exodus 3:14 NKJV) Essentially God was forecasting to the next generation, "Just as I was with those before you, becoming all that they needed, I will be the same to you."

Will it look the same? NO! For instance, God spoke to Moses through the burning bush, but God spoke directly to

Joshua. Moses was patient, a peacemaker, and he obediently provided water from the rock. Joshua, on the other hand, was a soldier. He was confrontational and instructed the people to dig their own wells. Moses was from the Levite tribe. Joshua was from the Ephraim tribe. The person and personality God chooses will change, but the provision and promise will stay the same from one generation to the next.

Moses	**Joshua**
Patient	Confrontational
Peacemaker	Soldier
Provided water from rock	Told people to dig wells
Levite Tribe	Ephraim Tribe
Diplomatic Leader	Slave

At times, I think about how different my father and I are. He is a great father, husband, and pastor. He is the guy who will tell anyone what they need to hear and it doesn't faze him if he is liked or not. He's never been intimidated or uncertain. He will tell the truth and I love him for it.

On the other hand, I have a strong desire for people to like me. Sometimes the need is so great it borderlines people pleasing. If I think someone doesn't like me, I may avoid ministering the truth. When I communicate, I often use humor to disarm people in an effort to open their hearts. When Dad ministers, he goes straight to the Word. We are two different people from the same DNA, but we still need the great I AM.

This was true with Moses and Joshua. While their personalities were vastly different, God used their exceptional talents for a specific purpose. Moses was a diplomatic leader who grew up in Pharaoh's house. Joshua was the son of Nun – Nun, as in nothing. He didn't come from a prominent family or background and his father was a slave. Moses got the children of Israel out of Egypt, but Joshua got Egypt out of the children of Israel. They wandered 40 years because they were never free in their spirits.

Maybe you can relate to this. You have been physically set free, but you have not been delivered. You are not in bondage, but you hold the scars and memories from your past. You just can't seem to get over who you were or what happened to you. You are in a wilderness place in your life. You have been set free, but you're still searching for what's next. The next part of your life is true deliverance. God wants you to move on, to move forward, and to move into your promise.

One of Joshua's greatest strengths was that he was not tied to a certain method. I believe the American church is stuck because we are tied to a methodology that was once effective but has expired. As we read on in the Bible, we will discover that Joshua was not tied to tradition. He didn't just do things differently to be different. He followed God for unique strategy and wisdom, but he opened his mind to let go of *what once was* so he could take people to *what could be.*

A good way to check your heart to see if you are tied to a certain methodology is to ask yourself, "Have I been critical of somebody's fruitful ministry because it's not my style or preference?" If it's producing Godly fruit, then it's of God – simple as that. We have to set aside our preferences for what God wants. Just think. If those who were following Joshua stopped him and said, "That's not what I'm used to. Moses always did it this way." Just as God was with Moses, He was with Joshua, and He is with *you.*

God is contemporary. From generation to generation, He is *our God.* This generation needs to know God may not function the same way with them as He did with generations before, but He is still God and His promises have not changed.

The Lord knows the injustices in our society. He sees the oppressed. He understands the hurt of religion. He recognizes the unfulfilled dreams in former generations and He understands the lack of mission in the church today. We have to realize *we* are God's answer to those problems!

THIS GENERATION NEEDS TO KNOW GOD MAY NOT FUNCTION THE SAME WAY WITH THEM AS HE DID WITH GENERATIONS BEFORE, BUT HE IS STILL GOD AND HIS PROMISES HAVE NOT CHANGED.

God desires to see change, not through political movements, not through rebellion, but through His Spirit! He urges us to continue the work started by those before us. Better yet, we have been carefully chosen, selected, ordained, gifted, and sent out to continue this work. Joshua answered this call. Think about this statement, "As I was with all the Christians up until now, so I will also be with you." What a declaration! "As I was with Peter, James, John, Paul, Moses, Joshua, Daniel, David, and Jesus, *so I will be with you.*"

God is in the business of succession. Jesus was the greatest example of this. When He left this earth, He proclaimed His mission to His disciples to continue what He started. Now, over 20 centuries later, we are continuing this mission. In every generation, God raises specific leaders to carry out this mission in the current context.

You may not realize it, but the church's present succession plan is not working. According to research from the Barna Group, 1.2 million people are leaving the church each year. That is 3,500 a day. In 2015, an estimated 10,000 churches closed their doors.

If there is ever a need for Joshuas to rise up, it's now. You are God's plan to lead people through the wilderness to reach the *promised land.* Stop looking around and start looking within. In my lifetime of ministry, I have heard people speculate where God is in times of need. People may ask why we have world hunger, a divided country, or broken families. The answer to this question is simple, but so challenging. God has chosen us, mankind, to make the difference. You may think you are waiting on God, but in reality He is waiting for you to realize how much He desires to see His Kingdom come and His will be done. That's why it is so imperative we understand God is contemporary. He is still eager for humanity to be in relationship with Him. The same love that was poured out on the cross over 2000 years ago is still alive and chasing after the 7 billion people on the planet. And His method of showing that love is through us.

God is raising up Joshuas of today to stand up and carry out the mission of Jesus Christ, just as Joshua carried out the mission of Moses. If your relentless passion is to see God move in a new way, a fresh way, a miraculous way, you are a modern-day Joshua. If you are teachable, moldable, and walk in humility with God, you are a modern-day Joshua. If you are willing to listen to God for wisdom and new strategies to reach and fulfill the mission of Christ, you are a modern-day Joshua.

<u>Pastor's Challenge:</u>

As I write this I wonder, "Do you know the 'I Am' and are you willing to step up as the Joshua generation did?"

If you are reading this book and you don't know Jesus Christ as your Lord and Savior, then you need to understand something. The thoughts, ideas, and truths I espouse in this book come from my belief that God loves us enough to send His Son to die for us.

I challenge you to read the first three chapters of the book of John to fully understand this. The Bible says, "For God so loved the world that He gave His only begotten Son, that whoever believes in Him should not perish but have everlasting life." (John 3:16 NKJV) God has offered us eternal life and a free life here on earth through His Son, Jesus.

"Oh, God, I pray for the one who is reading this book, but may not know you as Savior. May he or she come to understand all of the Gospel, the Good News, that while we were sinners in need of a savior, You reconciled us back to You through Your Son, Jesus, and that it's not Your will that any man shall perish. Amen." If you prayed this prayer or would like somebody to pray this with you, please reach out to me through my email at PastorLAinsworth@gmail.com. I would like to connect with you and help you start your relationship with Jesus.

The second part of my question was, "Are you willing to step up as the Joshua generation did? Are you willing to carry the mantle of those who have gone before you to bring God's Kingdom to earth?"

I believe we are in the generation that will see the promise of the Lord fulfilled. I believe many will come to know Christ and the dreams of those who have gone before us will be fulfilled. I believe we will rid ourselves of empty religion and pursue a vibrant relationship with God. And I believe that authenticity will prevail in our movement as we strive to be more like Him.

If you are willing to accept this challenge, then I want to pray for you and encourage you to read the rest of this book. The following chapters will provide guidance as we evaluate Joshua's life; key principles that marked his life and prepared him for the promise.

"God, I pray for all who read this book. May they realize that now is their time and you are calling them out. You have chosen them for such a time as this to be your voice to a lost, misguided generation. You, Lord, have a blessing for us on the other side of our obedience. Use the words of this book to bring glory to You! It is our ultimate desire to represent You here on earth."

Chapter 2

CONSECRATE YOURSELVES

"So Joshua made flint knives for himself, and circumcised the sons of Israel at the hill of the foreskins." (Joshua 5:3 NKJV)

During my lifetime, I've experienced a few ministry transitions. Maybe you can relate to a job transition. Usually the first advice I get from my new overseer is, "Don't change a whole lot right away. People are not used to change and may despise you for it." Well, obviously Joshua did not get the memo that big change was not a good idea for his first major move as the new leader.

To set the scene, Joshua embraced the role as leader of the Israelites. God directed him and the people that they were to follow Joshua. So, what was one of Joshua's first moves as commander and chief? He circumcised the men of Israel! What? Are you serious? Somebody didn't read, *How to Win Friends and Influence People*! You wouldn't think this was something a new leader should do. I can just see modern-day leaders pleading, "Stop! They aren't ready!" Or, "They will be angry with you."

So, why did Joshua circumcise the men? Circumcision began as a sign of covenant between God and Abraham. It then became a regular practice of the law as an outward expression of Israel's heart condition. It meant the circumcised person belonged to God.

Moses, who wrote the law through the inspiration of God, taught that men were to be circumcised. Leviticus 12:2-3 NKJV says, "Speak to the children of Israel, saying: 'If a woman has conceived, and borne a male child, then she shall be unclean seven days; as in the days of her customary impurity she shall be unclean. And on the eighth day the flesh of his foreskin shall be circumcised.'"

Moses knew about the first circumcision when God told Abraham to circumcise himself, his household, and his slaves as a sign of covenant with God. (Genesis 17:10-14) Yet, as a leader, Moses did not have the courage or desire to circumcise the young men during the 40 years they were in the wilderness.

There was actually a moment when God became angry with Moses and intended to kill him. That's right - kill him. He had not circumcised his own son, so his wife had to (Exodus 4). The wilderness generation was raised by a generation that sought comfort more than purpose. The children of Israel were marked stiff-necked whiners by God because they were seeking the promise of God and not God Himself. The Israelites

THE WILDERNESS GENERATION WAS RAISED BY A GENERATION THAT SOUGHT COMFORT MORE THAN PURPOSE.

behavior deteriorated and at one point He told Moses, "You can have the promise, but I will not go with you." (Exodus 33) Moses was a great leader, but he failed to pass on the importance of covenant and consecration to God. He placed comfort over growth. We have to realize God cares more about our growth than He does our comfort or emotions.

How many of you can relate? Does this sound familiar in our current situation? Think about it for a moment. From the time I was in middle school, I was told the key to success was to get good grades and work hard at a sport or other activity where I could earn a scholarship, so when I graduated I could go to college and get a degree. Once I received a degree, I could land a great-paying job, find a good wife, start saving for retirement, have 2 kids who are really cute, and provide the same opportunity for them. Sounds great right?

The American Dream in some ways is a trap. It's all about reaching some level of comfort with a nice job that comes with a nice salary. The problem with this model is that it does not leave room for the gifts, the callings, the trials, and the purposes of God.

We have been told to do everything we can to be comfortable and self-sufficient. In my experience, that system of thinking has left many of our generation wandering in the same wilderness as their parents. Don't get me wrong, God wants us to prosper. In Proverbs 10:22 we read, "The blessing of the Lord makes one rich, and He adds no sorrow with it." The problem is not the riches, but rather the motive to gain riches or the motive to reach the promised land.

Just a few years ago, one of my friends decided to make a big career move that shocked many people. He had been set up by his parents to work in the oil industry just like his dad. He went to school and had a job lined up right after graduated. Now if you are in a good position in the Texas oil industry, you are pretty much set for life. At an early age, he was making a great salary and on most people's scale he was very successful, but yet something was missing. He wasn't fulfilled. He had always wanted to be a teacher, and so when he left his lucrative position to be a rookie teacher for peanuts, everybody was perplexed. People tried to talk him out of it. He realized it's better to live a God ordained purpose than acquire some social status of success. Think of the many students that will benefit and reach their promised land for God because of his decision.

I think one of the issues hindering the American church is that we are teaching our kids to follow the American Dream rather than God's dream. The American Dream has been distorted. It used to be, anybody can do anything and has become, you can do anything but you must first… Well, there is one problem with this pressure that is imposed on the wilderness generation. Our elders want us to reach a place of comfort so they don't speak to the gifting, calling, and place God has called us to.

> **WE ARE TEACHING OUR KIDS TO FOLLOW THE AMERICAN DREAM RATHER THAN GOD'S DREAM.**

We have some members right now who have completed the cycle. They are coming out of colleges with degrees and bouncing from job to job wondering if this is all there is to life. They are lost. They are wandering in the wilderness, confused because they are supposed to have some sense of accomplishment, yet they are filled with disappointment.

God has called us to a life that is not driven by the idea of comfort. He has called us to see the beauty of trials and perseverance that leads to victory. I have observed some in our generation accept a much lower paying job because it spoke to their call – their gift, and it challenged them. Corporate America will suffer if it does not begin to understand this. We are not looking to build our 401Ks. We hunger for adventure, to make memories, and to be a part of something that has never been done before.

The sad part of all of this is we are a generation that has more education than any before and yet we are more lost than any generation. The lie that money, comfort or even knowledge, will lead to fulfillment has been exposed. The road to fulfillment and living out God's purpose all starts with the pain and the covenant of circumcision.

Am I suggesting all of today's wilderness generation males be circumcised right now? NO WAY! However, when the men who are our fathers, mentors, or role models are afraid of hurting us in the short-term, it creates long-term pain. Truett Cathy the founder of Chick-Fil-A says it this way, "It's easier to raise boys than it is to mend men." When a former generation tries to protect a younger one for the sake of comfort and safety, the emerging generation is really handicapped. They are hindered from receiving the promise of God.

Remember, it's through trials that we are perfected. James 1:2-4 NKJV reads, "My brethren, count it all joy when you fall into various trials, knowing that the testing of your faith produces patience. But let patience have *its* perfect work, that you may be perfect and complete, lacking nothing." Put another way, **if we are protected from trials, then we are incomplete lacking everything.**

God spoke to Joshua as the new, young leader of Israel and said that all of the young men were to be circumcised.

"For all the people who came out [of Egypt] had been circumcised, but all the people born in the wilderness, on the way as they came out of Egypt, had not been circumcised. For the children of Israel walked forty years in the wilderness, till all the people who were men of war, who came out of Egypt, were consumed, because they did not obey the voice of the Lord---to whom the Lord swore He would not show them the land which the Lord had sworn to their fathers that He would give us, 'a land flowing with milk and honey.'" (Joshua 5:5-6 NKJV)

Joshua did not want to go the easy way. He wasn't looking for comfort. He understood the children of Israel had to go through some discomfort in order to grow. This one act of obedience prepared them for continual success and a shift in their circumstances. Those who were going into the Promised Land had to be circumcised both physically and in their hearts. They needed to consecrate themselves, that is, they needed to declare themselves sacred, set apart for God's use.

They were saying we are Yours, Lord, our lives belong to You. I wonder, today have we truly declared Jesus the Lord of our lives? Have each of us made the decision to say, "My life will be marked by the Master. All I do will be a picture of His covenant with me."

What I have seen is that many in our generation merely want to be comfortable. They list God as just another category of their priority boards rather than allow Him to consume the total of their lives. Those people will continue to wander in the wilderness of their own minds if they are not willing to endure the pain of the 'cutting away.' The foreskin represents that part of our lives that is extra or excess, and not needed.

In Deuteronomy, we are taught to be circumcised in the heart. Deuteronomy 10:16 NKJV states, "Therefore circumcise the foreskin of your heart, and be stiff-necked no longer." So, in essence, get rid of your baggage.

Yet, the fact is, we cannot get rid of our baggage on our own. We need people in our lives to point out what should or should not be there. We need fathers and mentors who are not afraid to tell us the truth; men and women who are not afraid of hurting our feelings now because they are looking to save us some long-term pain later.

"For though you might have ten thousand instructors in Christ, yet you do not have many fathers; for in Christ Jesus I have begotten you through the gospel. Therefore, I urge you, imitate me." (1 Corinthians 4:15-16 NKJV)

In that scripture verse, Paul is saying we have many people who can teach us, but not many who care enough to father us. Think about this; how does a father teach? He may use words sometimes, but most of the time he teaches through his lifestyle as he brings us along. There are both good and bad things that I learned from my father – mostly good, I'd say. I have had the blessing of having godly parents.

When I was 13 my father took me to the country of Mongolia. It was a ministry trip for him because he was a pastor and evangelist, but I was just along for the ride, so, I was looking forward to the adventure. However, once we arrived, he told me, "Tomorrow will be your turn to speak."

"What?" I thought, "I'm 13, Dad! What do you think I have to say?" What he already knew and I didn't realize was that I had been watching him my whole life and through observation, I learned just by watching him live. Like any other 13-year-old preacher, I went straight to the book of Revelation. (No Joke!) From that moment on, I knew preaching was my calling. How did I know? Through a living example. I have seen my dad in some of his greatest moments in ministry and some of his worst.

As I grew up, I faced hurt, pain, and confusion. I remember being called out during church one morning to come sit on the front row because I was a distraction. Humiliated, I brooded, "Why am I being held to a higher standard? Why can't I be like all of the other kids?" My father knew the results of his discipline would be more important than my temporary feelings.

A father builds you for your future. He is not concerned about being your best friend. His goal is *not* to make you happy. He's looking to see you carry on a legacy. A father's desire for you is that you see the promised land. I have a few fathers now: my biological father, my grandfather, and some spiritual fathers. If your biological father is not a great example and you want one, I believe God can place men and women in your life to take that place. However, there's no benefit to you unless you are willing to follow them.

Right now our generation has many instructors. Just think, if we want to know something we can Google, Wiki, YouTube or study the information we have at our fingertips more than any other generation. We can listen to the latest and greatest preachers. We can hear amazing messages from amazing men and women of God, but they are not fathers. A father walks through life with you. He is not just a voice; he is an example.

A FATHER WALKS THROUGH LIFE WITH YOU. HE IS NOT JUST A VOICE; HE IS AN EXAMPLE.

Moses failed at fathering the children of Israel. He wanted them to live in comfort more than he wanted them to have a legacy. Though Joshua was a young leader, he became a father figure and mentor. He took the place of Moses in the wilderness generation's lives and through his actions he said, "I'm declaring that we are God's people through circumcision." The children of Israel became consecrated to God. They were His. They were holy.

Today's generation has not heard the holiness message. We love the grace message. Who doesn't? It is so much fun to preach on grace and yes, grace is the foundation of the message of Jesus. He died for us while He had no guarantee we would ever receive the free gift of salvation. Amazing! We have to realize grace has two sides. It's not just that Christ gave us salvation. He gave us power to live a holy life. As Peter said, "Be as obedient children, not conforming yourselves to the former lusts, as in your ignorance; but as He who called you is holy, you also be holy in all your conduct." (1 Peter 1:14-15 NKJV)

"No man should desire to be happy who is not at the same time holy. He should spend his efforts in seeking to know and do the will of God, leaving to Christ the matter of how happy he should be." - *AW Tozer*

In order to be holy, we have to cut off our former lusts and our former lifestyle. Holiness means to be set apart for God's use. This is the circumcision we must go through. It's what separates us from everybody else. We can't expect to reach a world we look and act like.

There is a difference between holiness and legalism. Legalism is trying to perform to get God's attention or to make ourselves feel superior to someone else through our own works. Holiness is the pursuit to be more like Christ, by denying ourselves and letting Him live in us. I believe the holiness message has dwindled because of legalistic application. For example, my wife and I have made it a point in our lives not to watch any movies or TV shows with nudity. This can be hard at times because friends will recommend a new TV show and I'm like, "Wow! I would love that story line. But God instilled a conviction in our hearts."

HOLINESS IS THE PURSUIT TO BE MORE LIKE CHRIST

Now, I can at times get judgmental toward others who do not have this same conviction, but the reality is that is not my job. My job as a Christian is to be obedient to the Lord in the convictions He gives me. I'm not to pass those convictions on to others. Some people have even turned away from the church because we started preaching rules or laws they must follow, instead of teaching them to want to become more like Christ. We must let Him take care of the convictions.

When I was growing up, I remember hearing pastors preach about how bad the internet was. They warned us because they thought it was from the devil and would cause the fall of all mankind. Well, some still say that is true, but the broader truth is that if we focus on rules more than principles, we fail to teach and train people how to function in life. For example, this book might be read through Kindle. It could be said that the same internet that is used to addict millions to pornography is also used to reach a person who needs Christ and is ready to reach their promised land. When we teach on holiness, we see a genuine life change from the inside out, not robots who have conformed to the legalism of religious acts.

But before the generation with Joshua could move on, it was necessary for them to go through the healing process. After we go through a time of pruning, God will always provide a time of healing. I have been through seasons of hurt, turmoil, and strain, but they were always followed by times of restoration. This is so important to understand; the healing time is as important as the pain or pressure. If you do not heal, you will not be able to fight the future battles the Lord has for you. For instance, a father or mentor might hurt your feelings when he tells you the truth about you. So, take time to reflect, rest, grow, become whole, talk it through, and take responsibility. Wisdom is knowing when to apply knowledge.

Once everybody had healed from circumcision, the Lord said to Joshua, "This day I have rolled away the reproach of Egypt from you." (Joshua 5:9 NKJV) That was a sacred moment for the children of Israel. They were finally free from Egypt. Their minds were officially delivered. I've seen many wander in a wilderness because they have never chosen to consecrate their lives to God, just like the Children of Israel. Christ has made freedom available but it's not until you accept that freedom by choosing to consecrate yourself to him. The Children of Israel were supposedly free but yet they still dealt with their past mentality because they never truly surrendered to God. True freedom comes when you fully trust the One that that has provided it.

As a church sometimes we confuse deliverance and freedom. The children of Israel were free from slavery, but they were not truly delivered. Think about it this way. We in America have been given certain freedoms through the sacrifices of many lives, but still we can be held down by addictions, mindsets, fear, and anxiety. Just because we have freedom does not mean we are walking in it. Once the children of Israel were circumcised, they were delivered. The reproach of Egypt was gone. Their past no longer had a foothold in their minds. We know we are truly delivered when we have peace. Peace is the fruit of deliverance. The enemy wants to torment us, and where he attacks us most is in our minds.

When we consecrate ourselves to God, we are no longer slaves to our past. We are no longer in survival mode. It's time to thrive! It's time to walk in victory! It's time to make an impact, and it's time to walk in your destiny! No more whining, complaining, bickering, or stiff-necked living. It's time to walk in the promise and life God has called us to live. There is freedom in submission!

Pastor's Challenge:

The greatest pursuit in life is to be holy like Christ. Do you truly desire holiness? Have you fallen into the trap of legalism? Ask the Lord to give you His convictions and see the benefits of a holy life.

If you do not have a mentor, a father, a leader that is willing to tell you the truth, I challenge you to find one very soon. Also, strive to be that kind of leader to others.

The greatest question I like to ask the fathers in my life is, "What do you see in my life that I can do better?" It is a great question and many times they will say, "Let me pray about it before I give you an answer." So, don't be disheartened and run away from the pain of growing... embrace it!

Feedback is the tool God uses to keep us from having to experience everything first hand. Maybe you're the person today that has been hurt by a good leader because you did not know how to handle his insight about your life. Maybe you didn't take time to process the fact that they were really trying to help you. Maybe you were defensive because you saw them as an enemy.

Perhaps you have hurts you haven't dealt with. Hurts and pain you're carrying from leaders because you have not dealt with what happened. God wants to bring healing. On the other side of your healing is victory! I do not trust a warrior who does not have scars. Scars serve as reminders of adversity. All extraordinary leaders have scars, and the greatest leader of all, endured for us the agony of 39 lashes and the holes in His hands and feet.

Chapter 3

THE MANNA IS GONE

"Then the manna ceased on the day after they had eaten the produce of the land; and the children of Israel no longer had manna, but they ate the food of the land of Canaan that year." (Joshua 5:12 NKJV)

How would you feel if everything you have eaten the past 40 years of your life is no longer available? Or how would you feel if God spoke to you every day a specific way and then the next day He decides to change it up? Change is difficult, but great leaders know how to flow and diversify for change. Your potential can be stifled by your willingness to change.

The manna ceased. Seems simple right? Well, think about this. Every single morning God provided the only food everyone under 40 had ever eaten... *manna.* Now it's gone?

First, they were circumcised, then while they were healing, all the manna disappeared. I'm sure they were freaking out at first! "What has happened? Has God left us? What has Joshua done? How are we going to survive? What is next?"

A new season requires a new provision. We can't live off 40-year-old victories. This is something all generations must learn. Many times I hear a group of older Christians begin to talk about the good ol' days when the music was a certain way or they heard a certain speaker or preacher they really liked. Now, don't get me wrong. I would love to hear, in person, some of the great preachers of the last centuries like; Martin Luther, John Calvin, Smith Wigglesworth, Billy Graham, or Martin Luther King. However, my greater interest is to hear the modern-day Billy Grahams, C. S. Lewises, Mother Theresas, or John Calvins.

If we keep idolizing the past, we will never be able to move forward. God's model for us is to honor the past and empower the future. Think about what Jesus did. He honored the old law and the prophets, but His focus was clearly on God's vision for the future. In Matthew 5 He said, "I didn't come to abolish the law (the old way) but I came to fulfill it."

> **IF WE KEEP IDOLIZING THE PAST, WE WILL NEVER BE ABLE TO MOVE FORWARD.**

Did you know Joshua is from the Hebrew name, *Yehoshu'a* meaning, "Yahweh is salvation"? Joshua's mandate was identical to the assignment of Jesus. He was not to dishonor the old, but rather carry out the mission.

Wow, I wish we could all grasp this. Imagine what we could accomplish if generations would stop competing and started completing each other. What if we locked arms together and joined forces. The wilderness generation needs the empowerment of the Moses generation and likewise the

Moses generation needs the Joshuas to complete the work. Let's stop idolizing the past and start energizing the future. We need to speak life into the potential of the wilderness generation, for we shall see the promise.

One of my great mentors, Tommy Barnett, always said, "The message is sacred, not the method." Manna was the provision in the wilderness, but in order to get out of the wilderness the children of Israel had to learn to toil the land. Essentially, they had to grow up. They needed to stop wandering and start working. Wow! What a picture of our current generation.

How many young people in western culture today are accustomed to being spoon fed or should I say, babied? We have been spoiled physically, emotionally, and spiritually.

> POLITICAL CORRECTNESS HAS COME AT THE COST OF MATURITY.

We are in the society of participation awards and we must not do anything to hurt somebody's feelings. Political correctness has come at the cost of maturity.

I remember when I was growing up, one of my best childhood friends had a really hard time with one thing that happened at his house. What was going on was atrocious. I'm not even sure I can tell you, but for the sake of making a point I will. Of course, I'm being sarcastic.

There were multiple times when while I was present, my dear friend yelled at his mother at the dinner table, "What have you done?" he hollered. Or sometimes he said, "Yuck! This is horrible!" All this because his mother had the audacity to buy the cheaper version of mac n' cheese – you know, the Great Value brand instead of Kraft? You must be wondering what she could have been thinking. Now, if you know me, you know I love mac n' cheese. That might be because my culinary skills are very limited. These are the types of problems the majority of our generation face.

Our greatest dilemmas are nothing compared to what generations in the past have suffered. I think about the past generation who survived the Great Depression. Many people literally rationed their food to make it and many parents went hungry in order to feed their children. The Cold War brought the daily terror of an atomic war and there were men, women and children who died fighting for equal rights in America.

These were just a few of the problems earlier generations endured. It is time the wilderness generation moves from being immature takers to being mature contributors. Maturity cannot come without hard work.

Joshua was leading a generation of inexperienced people. They had no idea how to toil the land or the goodness it could produce. They did not have work ethic and had no need for it. I have seen parents try to give their kids what they didn't have. That's an honorable thing to do, but we handicap our children's future when we don't teach them the value of hard work. When I was 12 and 13, I remember going to my great grandma's house to pull weeds for hours and hours. I can still remember the first time she told me if I worked hard, she would pay me well. I thought, "Man, this is my moment to buy that new BB gun I wanted." After a full day's work, she gave me three dollars. Yes, three dollars! Now remember, this is my great grandma who was in her

80s. To her that seemed like a good wage, but what I earned was more valuable than money, it was work ethic. In James 2 it says, "Faith without works is dead." So then faith with works is alive. You cannot expect God to deliver new provision without a strong work ethic.

It's sad when I think about it. For 40 years they ate the same thing every day. The wilderness generation had no idea about the amazing taste of a juicy watermelon on a hot day or the sweet taste of a fresh orange in the morning. And oh, my goodness, how can I forget a juicy steak? I mean their taste buds were so limited!

New Hunger

Spiritually, I believe our taste buds have been desensitized because we have not spiritually tasted the fullness of the promised land. We have been fed a bland Christianity that promises comfort rather than a deep satisfying relationship with a loving God. I can remember distinct times in my life when I had revelations while studying certain principles of life. When the light bulb came on, I remember the first time I felt the presence of the Holy

Spirit. It was an all-encompassing peace that was indescribable.

Also, I remember the first time I wasn't just sorry I was caught in sin, but rather I was sorry for the sins themselves and I felt the grace of God cover my life. This is the promised land. These are the deep things of God. I remember preaching my first message and thinking that somehow it felt so natural, like breathing, like I found what I was meant to do. Can you relate? Have you had God moments in your life that you will never forget?

I remember one day when I was helping my son build Legos and he kept insisting that he do it himself. So, like a good dad, I sat back and watched, waiting eagerly to help. The moment he asked for help, we had the greatest time. His response after we finished was, "Look, Daddy, at what I built!" To this day, he loves constructing Legos together. The revelation hit me. How many times have I tried to show off what "I built" to my Heavenly Father when in reality without Him it would have been impossible?

There are so many instances in my life where a revelation of God hits home and my spiritual taste buds come alive like the first time I tasted some food. The light clicked on, "Oh, this is what this tastes like. This is what people were talking about."

We can never have these moments when we depend on being fed from everyone around us. A new season requires a new hunger, new dedication, and a new discipline that results in new tastes. Your appetite will dictate your direction in life.

YOUR APPETITE WILL DICTATE YOUR DIRECTION IN LIFE.

New provision means new victory. God told Joshua that the children of Israel could eat from the land of Canaan. They would now be working and toiling for their food. God was preparing them for their promise. The preparation for your promise is just as important as the promise itself.

Moses' victory was freeing people from slavery. He went to Pharaoh and said, "Let my people go." He believed for freedom, he trusted God, and he saw God move through mighty works. When you hear about the plagues that hit Egypt and think about what a great testimony they were; water turned into blood, frogs, lice, flies and wild animals, diseased livestock, boils, thunderstorms of hail and fire, locusts, darkness for three days, and the killing of all the firstborn males – all of these miracles for the sole purpose of getting the children of Israel out of slavery.

Just imagine the freeing of over two million slaves. What a victory that was! Slavery was all that generation had known, but they followed Moses into the wilderness. On their way out, they were chased by chariots, by Pharaoh's army. They looked at Moses and said, "We should have stayed in Egypt."

This gives us a good idea of whom Moses was leading – people who begged for freedom but did not want to pay the price for it. Have you ever met someone who wanted a trophy, but never wanted to run the race, much less prepare for the race? Be careful of people who want the reward without the process, for they will always be the ones complaining about what they don't have.

One of the fair terms imposed on millennials is, "entitled." The attitude of entitlement is being owed something not earned. Entitlement has been ingrained in the wilderness generation because they have not been taught the sacrifices made for the many benefits they have received. To counter an entitlement attitude, we have to teach gratitude and the importance of hard work. **It's impossible to be grateful and entitled at the same time.**

God worked another miracle for the Israelites. He dried up the Red Sea and then destroyed Pharaoh's army. To read the full story, check out Exodus 14. They were free! Not only were the children of Israel released from their captors; the captors were dead. The enemy was cut off, however, the issue was that their minds were not free.

The wilderness generation watched as their parents, their mentors, and their grandparents were physically set free from slavery, but their minds were still bound by their experience and perspective. Our perspective determines our view of reality. Jesus said it this way, "But if your eye is bad, your whole body will be full of darkness." (Matthew 6:23 NKJV) Jesus wasn't referring to our physical eye, but rather our perspective and our vision for life.

Joshua was in a position to take a generation into true freedom, but they had to fight for it. They worked the land and engaged their faith. God is looking for a generation willing to fight, walk by faith, move with power, and speak with boldness. We have seen the unfulfilled dreams of our predecessors, and we have watched as a generation before us whined and developed a hard heart toward God. But we have to shake off antagonistic history. We need to be thankful for our birthright and walk into the promise He has given us.

New Strategy

In Joshua 7, we see the famous story of Jericho. Joshua took on his first battle since the people were circumcised and the manna had ceased. Take note here because something amazing was about to happen. From this story we see that for 7 days, all of Israel marched around Jericho then on the

7th day, they shouted and blew the trumpets and a miracle happened... the walls fell down!

What a great victory, but I think in the midst of the miracle we might be missing the message. It was a new season for the wilderness generation. They consecrated themselves and prepared to eat off the land, but they had to learn that in a new season comes new strategy.

Maybe one of Joshua's generals eluded to the success of Moses during battle by the raising of his rod. Maybe we should try that because this idea of marching with trumpets does not sound promising.

In a new season, with a new vision, the new provision comes with new strategy. I believe God is going to give specific directions to the wilderness generation regarding how to accomplish His will on this earth. If we are willing to trust Him fully, we will see the victory of the Lord.

God wants to give millennials a new strategy, and I believe we are ready for it. 35% of millennials have already started businesses to supplement their income. We are looking for new ways of provision. There is a spirit of entrepreneurship from inside this generation. What it takes is a Joshua to listen to the strategy God wants to provide and have the boldness to obey. Just think about the strategy God gave Jericho; march around for 7 days and then make a lot of noise. Doesn't make sense right? Well a God idea will trump a good idea every time.

New Provision

There is a movement among America to encourage people to shop and sell locally, to support small businesses and entrepreneurs. Why is that? Because our generation loves the personal touch of a local business. Not only do we like the personal touch, but we love convenience. If you don't believe that then ask Blockbuster.

I love the story of Uber and an excerpt from their website. "On a snowy Paris evening in 2008, Travis Kalanick and Garrett Camp had trouble hailing a cab. So they came up with a simple idea—tap a button, get a ride. What started as an app to request premium black cars in a few metropolitan areas is now changing the logistical fabric of cities around the world. Whether it's a ride, a sandwich, or a package, we use technology to give people what they want, when they want it." This is a picture of new manna, a new provision. Uber today is valued at over 68 billion dollars. It started with two guys who decided to think outside the box.

New provision starts with a desire to move from daily manna to abundance. Yes, God wants us to have abundance. The meaning of "the land of milk and honey" means all good things. God is taking us to a place that has all good things. He desires for you to have more than enough, not for waste, but for the Kingdom's gain.

This wilderness generation has become leery of the "prosperity Gospel" but many of them don't understand the blessing of God. We see big pastors or evangelists who have large amounts of money and we begin to judge them. How can you serve God and have worldly possessions? Well, the thing we have to understand is that it's ok to have things just as long as the things don't have us. God never meant for us to live on this earth and suffer. From the beginning in Genesis, God told us to subdue and have dominion over the earth. Does that sound like somebody who is suffering? Where we have gone astray in the past is with Christian leaders who have manipulated people to suffer so they could prosper. That's not God's way. His desire is that all of us should prosper. Joshua was leading the wilderness generation into their own land so they could have their own nation, so they would not lack anything. The prosperity of Joshua meant the prosperity of everyone. "A good *man* leaves an inheritance to his children's children," (Proverbs 13:22) We should not be afraid to prosper. Your blessing will be a part of your legacy.

Are we ready to move past just getting by into having more than enough? Rick Warren, who pastors Saddleback Church and is a world renowned author and speaker, is a great example of how to view God's provision and abundance, so much so, he gives away ninety percent of his income to help out those less fortunate. Here is a blurb from a recent interview that Beliefnet.com did with him:

Kay and I became reverse tithers. When we got married 30 years ago, we began tithing 10%. Each year we would raise our tithe 1% to stretch our faith: 11% the first year, 12% the second year, 13% the third year. Every time I give, it breaks the grip of materialism in my life. Every time I give, it makes me more like Jesus. Every time I give, my heart grows bigger. And so now, we give away 90% and we live on 10%. That was actually the easy part, what to do with the money--just give it away, because I'm storing up treasures in heaven.

If God can trust that He can get something *through* you, He will get it *to* you. Olivia and I sit down many times throughout a year and talk about our budget. Usually at first it starts out with where we are financially and where our money is going and why it is going there. At the end of our budget meetings, we begin to dream... what we could do for others with what we have and what we are praying to gain in the future. Our

IF GOD CAN TRUST THAT HE CAN GET SOMETHING *THROUGH* YOU, HE WILL GET IT *TO* YOU.

vision for our provision is to be able to bless others. Every year of our marriage, we have seen God give an increase, and every year we increase our giving.

Pastor's Challenge:

So my question to you is: have you been served a bland Christianity? Are you ready to taste the fullness of the promise? If you are ready, then are you open to working hard for new provision? Are you willing to listen to the voice of God on new strategies? Are you willing to honor the past and empower the future? Can you be trusted with an abundance?

It's with great excitement that I ask these questions because I believe the Holy Spirit is speaking to you. In this moment, dreams are coming alive and you are ready to move forward. You are ready to lead *the transformation.*

In the next section of this book we are going to talk about the preparation Joshua experienced to become the leader of God's people. The *preparation* is just as important as the *promise.*

THE PREPARATION

"Failing to prepare is preparing to fail." - John Wooden

My very first real job, where I wasn't just working for a family member, was at my favorite fast food restaurant, Taco Villa, in Lubbock, Texas. Now you must understand something about Taco Villa. This place is amazing! If you love Tex-Mex then you know what I'm talking about. I could go on and on about how great Taco Villa is but that's not the goal of this book. Perhaps that's what my next book will be about. I'm kidding!

Food prep was my responsibility. I worked evenings after school and I prepped all the food for the next day. I shredded cheese, made salsa, set the beans to cooking overnight and cut tomatoes. When the team came in the next day everything would be ready for them to serve. In other words, they would be set up to win. As Benjamin Franklin said, “By failing to prepare, we are preparing to fail.”

Preparation sets you up to win in life. If you have no preparation you cannot win. Preparation is what separates those who are called from those who are chosen. We are all called to greatness but not all of us get chosen. To be chosen depends on how you answer the call.

> PREPARATION IS WHAT SEPARATES THOSE WHO ARE CALLED FROM THOSE WHO ARE CHOSEN.

Joshua became the leader of the Wilderness Generation. What set him apart from everybody else was his preparation. “After the death of Moses, the servant of the Lord, it came to pass that God spoke to Joshua, the son of Nun, Moses’ assistant, saying…” (Joshua 1 NKJV)

I love the way the Bible introduces Joshua, First, it is noted that he is the son of Nun. Nun is his father's name, nothing special. Do you come from Nun? I think many of us think, "God can't use me because I'm not special. I don't come from a great family or some exalted background."

Second, Joshua is defined as an assistant. Now, I don't know about you but my flesh is not a big fan of the word, assistant. I like titles like CEO, boss, El Capitan, the beast, or even the leader...but assistant? Come on now! However, God is showing us that to lead we must first become an assistant. What does an assistant do? He assists. He serves. He watches and learns how the leader performs his job. He does whatever is asked of him.

Your preparation is directly connected to how well you serve. The greatest leader to ever walk on this earth, Jesus Christ said, "Just as the Son of Man did not come to be served, but to serve, and to give His life a ransom for many." (Matthew 20:28 NKJV)

If Jesus, who was God in the flesh, came to serve people then who are we if we don't? Joshua was one of the greatest servants in the Bible and in this book we see three qualities of his preparation. He learned how to follow before he led. He understood the role of spiritual authority, and he had a positive attitude. Some of you might want to skip over these chapters and turn directly to the end, the good part. I challenge you not to do that. If you don't learn about preparation you will never see the end. You will never see the promise fulfilled.

Chapter 4

BECOMING A FOLLOWER

"So Moses arose with his assistant Joshua, and Moses went up to the mountain of God."

(Exodus 24:13 NKJV)

I am personally a huge fan of leadership books, they inspire me to dream bigger, be more effective, and learn from others who have gone before me. There are literally thousands of spiritual and secular leadership books out there. They provide valuable insight on how to manage companies, have a compelling vision, structure for growth, and care for the people we lead. Something missing from many of these books is teaching the importance of following.

Learning to be a follower is a lost art in most cultures. We act more like employees than followers. We behave more like a congregation than followers. Jesus created followers, not mere believers. If you ask most people today if they BELIEVE in God, they would say yes, but the real question is, "Do you FOLLOW God?" In rabbinic times, the Jewish culture established a system to develop followers or in other words, disciples.

Here is a quick synopsis of discipleship in the Jewish culture as the Mishnah describes the educational system for Jewish children. At the age of 5, a child is declared fit for the scripture and allowed to study. At the age of 12, each one will have attempted to memorize the whole Torah, which is the first five books of the Bible. The elite students will then move on to secondary school, where they will learn how to make their own rabbinic interpretations as they study the rest of the Old Testament.

This education was vital since every family didn't have a physical copy of the Old Testament. Next, a few of the very outstanding students would ask to follow a rabbi. Those students would ask to be a part of the Talmidim; translated, that means disciple or follower. The rabbi only chose a few to follow him, because in the system a rabbi is not just a teacher, but a mentor.

The student would follow him and take notes of everything he did and taught. The students became the legacy of the rabbi. They would carry out his understanding and interpretation of the scripture. When Peter and Andrew first saw Jesus, they went after Him. "Then Jesus turned, and seeing them following, said to them, 'What do you seek?' They said to Him, 'Rabbi' (which is to say, when translated, Teacher), 'where are You staying?'" (John 1:38 NKJV)

Over fifteen times the word, Rabbi is used in the New Testament. The disciples were not just looking for something to believe in, they were looking for someone to follow. Now, we know Jesus' disciples were not in the talmidim. They were not the best of the best students. They had moved on to other occupations. We don't know all of their occupations, but we do know some were fishermen and Matthew was a tax collector. The point is, Jesus did not just come for the best. He came to disciple everyone who is willing. He's not just looking for the smartest, not only the strong, or the intelligent, popular, famous, or rich.

> THE DISCIPLES WERE NOT JUST LOOKING FOR SOMETHING TO BELIEVE IN, THEY WERE LOOKING FOR SOMEONE TO FOLLOW.

Anybody can come to Jesus. How amazing is that? Jesus has the power to take your ordinary and give it a little extra to make you extraordinary! One of my favorite verses is in Acts 4:13 (NKJV), "Now when they saw the boldness of Peter and John and perceived that they were uneducated and untrained men, they marveled. And they realized that they had been with Jesus."

Here, Luke tells the story of Peter and John's arrest for preaching the Gospel after Jesus ascended to heaven. They were arrested by the Sanhedrin; the brightest and best of the religious society, the chosen ones. They questioned and examined Peter and John. Then, after their interrogation, they concluded Peter and John were ordinary, uneducated men with nothing special about them except for one thing... they had been with Jesus.

Can you relate? Do you feel ordinary or uneducated? Do you feel unworthy? Do you feel like you have been overlooked? God specializes in using the ordinary to do the supernatural.

GOD SPECIALIZES IN USING THE ORDINARY TO DO THE SUPERNATURAL.

If you want God to do some supernatural things with your life, then you have to become a follower. You have to take on His way of life. He sent His Son to give us the ultimate example to follow so we can walk in His footsteps and carry out His legacy here on earth. If you have merely been a believer sitting on the sidelines, it's time to get off the bench and become a follower. Becoming a follower is where the promise is fulfilled.

Long before Jesus came, Joshua was a follower. Joshua prepared himself for promotion. How? By following Moses. He went wherever Moses asked him to go. He was an assistant before he was a leader. The greatest leaders are those who know how to follow.

I remember times in Bible school where I prayed prayers like, "God, I just want to be used by You, and I will do whatever it takes. Just tell me what to do." Usually what followed was one of my mentors gave me a menial task to do, but it was my chance to be a follower. **I learned God would answer my big prayers with small daily instructions.**

Now when I get frustrated or think I am not where I want to be and look back on those times, I remember what it's all about. It's about following! Even as I am writing this I am not the senior pastor of my church. I am an associate pastor. In other words, I am an assistant to the pastor. I follow my senior pastor.

If you are too big for the small things, then you are too small for the big things. It's the details of life that separate us. Sound like platitudes? Yes, but they are true. If you think about your career, you can easily say that all the people in your career field have all the knowledge they need to be successful. It's usually how a person follows that separates him from the whole and causes him to excel and go above and beyond to greater heights.

"You can have everything in life you want, if you will just help other people get what they want."

- Zig Ziglar

Many people think *assistant* is a bad word. They don't want to be an assistant, they want to be the leader. The idea of an assistant's role is to help someone else accomplish their vision and their work. That may sound unappealing.

I have seen a few people who were really good at assisting, some who I have worked with and others I have seen from afar. There were many assistants in the Bible. To name a few; the disciples, David when he was his father's shepherd, Joseph, Elisha, and Jesus when He first came onto the scene assisting His mom during a wedding. Jesus' first 30 years were really spent assisting His father and mother.

Many times as you follow God, He will put leaders in your life you are to follow and assist. Joshua was called by God to lead the children of Israel into the Promised Land, but before he reached that position, he followed Moses.

How well you follow your leaders will determine your destination. I have worked for three megachurches and helped plant one church, and in all four of these experiences, I have had great favor because I have learned the importance of following.

Now, have I got it all figured out? No way, but I have seen the hand of God move in my life because of the way I have assisted my leaders. In my lifetime, I have learned three great qualities that make a good assistant.

1. ***An assistant anticipates his leader's needs and desires before they arise.*** This is one of the greatest qualities somebody can have. It speaks of chemistry between the leader and follower. Too many times we are in a paralyzing position in our lives because we are waiting for somebody to come up to us and tell us what to do, but a good follower takes initiative. This requires that the assistant takes the time to watch and observe the leader. To anticipate needs, you must first catch the heart of a leader.

2. ***An assistant comes early and stays late.*** We see in Exodus 24; Joshua arises early with Moses to go up on the Hill. If you continue reading you see he stayed up there with him 40 days and 40 nights. I've heard many people ask how they can be promoted. They want to know how they can walk into the next spiritual level of their lives, but they are usually the ones who are late to arrive and the first to leave.

Some of the greatest mentoring moments of my life were when I came early or stayed later to grab hold of something great. Elijah told Elisha three times to stay back, for what reason we don't know, but some say Elijah wanted to see how bad Elisha wanted the promotion; to see how much he was willing to sacrifice to receive the double portion. Elisha didn't know promotion was coming. He was just trying to be a good assistant.

3. ***An assistant has his own relationship with God.*** This is so key because I've seen so many unhealthy assistants who allowed their relationship with their leader to become more important than their relationship with God. They made their leader their God. If the leader's emotions swayed or he went through painful temptations, so did they.

God has called us to carry the spiritual weight of our leaders, but not the personal weight. When an assistant has his own personal relationship with God, he will at times be the one to minister to the leader when he needs it the most. Like Noah's sons when he got drunk, some covered him up while others freaked out. Your leaders will fail and they will have moments of weakness. This is when you are called upon to minister to them.

When you become a great assistant – a great follower – your leader will see your potential. In Numbers 13:16, Moses changed Joshua's name from Hosea to Joshua. Hosea means salvation, and Joshua means God is salvation. This seems like a small difference, but when you start to look at the bigger picture this was a life changing moment for Joshua. Moses was speaking over Joshua's life that God was going to bring him salvation and deliverance. Not only was God going to deliver Joshua, but He was going to use Joshua to bring deliverance to the people.

Great leaders will speak life over you, prophesy to your future, and speak things into existence. If nobody has expressed it yet, dear reader, I believe in you. I am calling you a Joshua. God is your salvation and He is going to use you to lead people out of the wilderness and into the promise of God. God is going to use you to do great and mighty acts for His glory. Your past does not determine your future. Your value is not shaped by your mistakes and you are not a mistake. You were God's idea. You are His workmanship, created in His image to triumph in Holy Spirit power. We have an enemy that seeks to intimidate, lie, and steal our value and identity, but I declare over your life, "You are a Joshua. God is your deliverance from the evil one and this world."

YOU ARE A JOSHUA. GOD IS YOUR DELIVERANCE FROM THE EVIL ONE AND THIS WORLD.

There is a little scripture in Exodus 33:11 where Joshua is mentioned as an afterthought. "So the Lord spoke to Moses face to face, as a man speaks to his friend. And he would return to the camp, but his servant Joshua the son of Nun, a young man, did not depart from the tabernacle."

Let me give you the context of the verse so it will better help you understand the heart of Joshua. Moses would go outside the camp when he heard the Lord calling him. There, he set up a tent which was called the meeting tent. When the people saw this they became very excited to hear what the Lord was saying to Moses. It was their connection point to God. They would lay prostrate and silent until Moses came out and told them what God had spoken. After this great moment, everybody would go on about their business or follow the direction God had given, but not Joshua. He stayed back in the tent. Why? What did he have to gain? I believe Joshua stayed back because he knew the secret of Moses' success. Joshua could also hear God. Moses spoke to God face to face. Joshua had that desire in his heart. He didn't want to overtake Moses, rather he wanted to be in God's presence.

When we become better followers, we not only learn what a leader does but who he is. The most valuable things I have learned in my life from leaders are things I caught, not the things I was taught. I listened and watched. Joshua caught the spirit of Moses because he was willing to be an assistant. I have two children and sometimes I am amazed by how much I sound like my parents. We have adopted a famous saying from my parents for our kids, "You are a winner, not a whiner." If you can, please, pray for my children to catch this! I'm kidding, but not really!

My point is, I think the wilderness generation is looking for mentors. We are waiting for somebody to come up to us and have a change our name experience. That's not going to happen until you are willing to be an assistant and you make moves to follow somebody you admire.

We are waiting to be discovered. But understand, you can't move forward until you make the most of where you are and use what is in your hand. Follow the leaders in your life right now. Moses saw something in Joshua long before he changed his name. He saw something in Joshua before setting him up for succession.

When Elijah prepared to put the mantle on Elisha, what was Elisha doing? He was plowing the field. If you want a double portion to come your way, then get busy plowing your field. When Samuel came to anoint the new

IF YOU WANT A DOUBLE PORTION TO COME YOUR WAY, THEN GET BUSY PLOWING YOUR FIELD.

king, they had to go find David in the field shepherding. All these men have something in common. They were busy following God and serving men when their divine moment came. Stop looking for your big break and start being faithful where you are. Set roots. Get planted.

Everyone wishes they could travel the world and live life to the fullest. Don't get me wrong, I love to travel. My famous quote is, "You never regret spending money on a memory being made with the ones you love." But your dreams won't work unless you do. You can have all the aspirations and ideas you want but without backing down and getting started, your dreams will be just that... a dream.

I've always had a dream to be in full-time ministry. I think it's funny how many people view pastors. They think we sit around all day studying the Word of God, praying, and floating around following God's Spirit. Why do I find that funny? Well, as I write this, I just finished 2 hours of vacuuming, taking out trash, setting up chairs, praying for a man who came to our office out of the blue looking for a job, and helping a mother in the church load up a baby swing and it's only 10:00 a.m.!

Now, don't get me wrong, I'm not complaining. I am blessed to be where I am, but to get here, I volunteered over 60 hours a week for 5 years before I ever received a small paycheck from a church. When Olivia and I first got married, she worked at Starbucks while I worked for a roofing company and at the airport as a valet. On top of all that, I directed a children's ministry without remuneration. I'm not looking for a pat on the back, but it was in those times I learned the power of serving and being a good follower.

The seeds you plant as a follower now you will reap as a leader later. What seeds are you planting right now in your job? What seeds are you planting with your parents? Good or bad, you will reap that harvest.

Pastor's Challenge:

My question to you is, "Are you a follower of Jesus Christ?" Before you answer, really consider what it means to be a follower, to take on the lifestyle of that leader. I'm not asking you if you are saved or if you believe in Jesus. What I'm asking you is, are you a follower? Have you dedicated your life to the legacy of Jesus? If you are not following Jesus right now, I challenge you to begin today. Begin to see Him as your Rabbi. Remember, it's not about how smart, rich, or powerful you are. It's about how much you are willing to surrender.

Are you being a good assistant to the leaders God has positioned in your life? How you assist will determine how you lead in the future. Perhaps you are currently in a situation where you don't have a godly leader or somebody that you respect. Think about David. He served Saul even though Saul was trying to kill him. God has not forgotten you and He will reward openly what you do in secret. Don't stop doing what got you where you are. Continue to be a good assistant. Continue to follow well.

Chapter 5

VICTORY THROUGH SUBMISSION

"And so it was, when Moses held up his hand, that Israel prevailed; and when he let down his hand, Amalek prevailed." (Exodus 17:11 NKJV)

Every day we are faced with the choice of compromise for a temporary gratification or sacrifice for a much greater reward. God has provided truth for us to live by, or a true north as I call it. If we look at our life like a compass and if we are off even a couple of degrees, we will end up at a destination we never intended.

The Amalekites were the descendants of Esau. Esau is known for trading away his birthright for a bowl of soup to his brother Jacob. The Amalekites represent a spirit that desires temporary satisfaction at the cost of eternal rewards. Let's look at this metaphorically. Joshua had to be under the right authority to defeat the enemy of compromise. This was a powerful teaching moment for Joshua.

The Israelites were fighting the Amalekites. Joshua was leading the charge, fighting his heart out while Moses was up on the mountain with his staff (rod) and two assistants Aaron and Hur. When the staff was raised, Israel was winning. When it was lowered, they started to lose. We are talking about lives hanging in the balance of Moses' arm strength! When Moses got tired and sat down on a rock, Aaron and Hur held his arms up to secure the victory. There are so many teaching points in this chapter, but right now I want to focus on one – Joshua's role.

Joshua's role in this instance was to follow his leader's command to gather men and fight Amalek. Now here's a truth: the victory is not won by the most effort, *it is won by being under the right authority.*

THE VICTORY IS NOT WON BY THE MOST EFFORT, *IT IS WON BY BEING UNDER THE RIGHT AUTHORITY.*

Young leaders don't like that word... authority. Maybe you have been hurt by a leader. Maybe people have used their authority to manipulate you. Maybe you have even had those above you try to lead you somewhere they have never been themselves. In life you will have some really great leaders who will teach you invaluable life lessons. You will also have some bad leaders who you will have the opportunity to learn just as much from. You will learn who you don't want to be and the harm bad leadership can cause, but you will still be asked to honor and respect the position God has given them.

We must come to the understanding that we can be the most disciplined, the strongest, most talented, and yet we will never reach our potential until we align ourselves with the right authority.

A person who is not submitted is dangerous. When we are not submitted, our vision of God and those God has put in a leadership position over us is distorted, and we are dangerous to the Kingdom.

"A Christian dangerous to the kingdom?" you ask. Yes, because those who don't submit have the potential to bring division. Like my pastor, Lynton Turkington, says, "Di means two, so division means two visions." There cannot be unity when the congregation doesn't share the same vision. I have seen first-hand, some of the most amazing Christians who are frustrated with their lives because they know they are not living up to their full potential, but don't know why. They are talented, anointed men and women of God, but because they have refused to submit to the authority placed over them, they have never achieved what God has in store for them.

We must realize that *authority* is delegated. We are not self-appointed. Ultimate authority on this earth is the Lord's and He delegated it to mankind. Adam and Eve messed that up for us in the Garden, so God sent us a "second Adam" (1

Corinthians 15:45) to fix what the first one messed up. Therefore, He sent His Son, Jesus, to take back the authority that was given away.

It's through Jesus that we have authority here on earth. It's at the sound of His name that the demons tremble. So, I want to warn you not to follow leaders who don't submit to Jesus' authority and His teaching. The Bible warns against false prophets. You can recognize a false prophet by two things. First, check out the fruit they produce and secondly, check out what they teach. Does it line up with what Jesus taught? If you are under a false prophet, I urge you to leave your current situation and get under the right authority.

A police officer can stand in front of traffic, stick out his hands, and everybody will stop. It's not because he has the physical power to stop the cars, it's because he has the authority. We do not have the physical strength or wits to fulfill the promise God has placed in our life, but we can do all things with the authority given to us.

When is the last time you exercised your godly authority here on Earth? Joshua was in a battle and he knew he was going to win if Moses' arms were up. If God's authority was at work for him, it didn't matter how many men were against him. It didn't matter what kind of weapons he was fighting with. He knew that when God is for you nobody can stand against you.

Just once, Jesus was documented as being amazed, as being speechless. In the book of Matthew, a Centurion, the title given to a captain in the Roman army who led about 80 men, came to Jesus on behalf of his servant. The story reads,

> *Now when Jesus had entered Capernaum, a centurion came to Him, pleading with Him, saying, "Lord, my servant is lying at home paralyzed, dreadfully tormented. And Jesus said to him, I will come and heal him.*
>
> *The centurion answered and said, Lord, I am not worthy that You should come under my roof. But only speak a word, and my servant will be healed. For I also am a man under authority, having soldiers under me. And I say to this one, Go, and he goes; and to another, Come, and he comes; and to my servant, Do this, and he does it. When Jesus heard it, He marveled," (Matthew 8:5-13 NKJV)*

Let's look at this for a moment. A man who understands Authority has awed Jesus, the son of God, the miracle worker, the perfect man. How? He finally met somebody who understood the power of authority.

Many of us have asked Jesus to do something in our lives, but it has not come to pass because we don't truly believe in the authority of Christ. Your victory is determined by your understanding of God's authority at work in your life. We fall into this trap that if God speaks to us, we want confirmation from everybody and everything that He has spoken. We will make wild requests, testing to see if what God has spoken is real. God was amazed by the faith of the Centurion because he didn't need any confirmation. He took God's word to the bank. He knew he could count on it. You don't need three people to confirm what God has spoken, or somebody to prophesy it. God said it. It's done if you believe!

Our generation is notorious for rebelling against and undermining authority. We don't like the idea of submission. Today's wilderness generation wants to be their own boss. They don't want to take orders.

Why does this happen? I believe three key factors play into this; **pride, impatience, and rebellion**. Now, these three can seem like very generic issues that a young leader might face, but I have seen how they can affect and delay the call of God on a life.

Pride

Let's look at each one in depth. One Scripture verse says about pride, "The Lord detests all the proud of heart. Be sure of this: They will not go unpunished." (Proverbs 16:5 NIV)

God hates pride, plain and simple, yet we all deal with it in some form or way. Some of the greatest assets of a young leader are a new perspective and a fresh passion. These are forces that can drive you to initiate change for the Kingdom of God, however, many times this passion and new perspective can lead to a place of pride.

It's so easy to start thinking that your way is the right way or the only way. For instance, you might start to think you are wiser or smarter than those in earlier generations who laid the path before you. God instilled innovation and creativity in us so that we can fulfill our Kingdom purposes, but those purposes will always be in the context of our being under the right authority.

Pride says, "I don't need anybody else." Pride despises feedback and demands the complete total of what he thinks belongs to him. The prodigal son in Luke 15 asked for his inheritance, what ultimately would belong to him one day. The mindset that led to his decision was, give me what's mine. I know better and I don't need anybody else. We see how the story unfolds and he lost everything. All of us can relate to having pride.

The greatest distance between two people is your pride. We are furthest away from God when we are acting in pride. I believe we fall into sin when we live like we don't need God. Some have the attitude of adding God into their lives like an extra ingredient rather than acknowledging He is the source of everything good in their lives. God is not an

> **THE GREATEST DISTANCE BETWEEN TWO PEOPLE IS YOUR PRIDE.**

additive. He is the sole reason and purpose we exist on this earth.

Impatience

Next, take a look at impatience which is the *lack* of patience. I can hear my dad saying this again right now, "If you abort the process, you abort the mission." Patience is a sign of maturity. A prayer I have prayed throughout my life is, "Lord, give me spiritual maturity well beyond my years."

My grandfather, Emory Cassell, has been very blessed in his business and because of it, he has made a huge impact for God by supporting hundreds of missionaries and missions organizations. I remember asking him one day what made him so successful. His answer to my question was so simple it almost made me angry. I thought, "There has to be more to success than what he is sharing with me." The more I thought about it, however, the more I realized what God was trying to show me.

My grandfather's answer was, "Faithfulness". Essentially, that's staying the course, persevering, not giving up when everybody else does. When I get impatient, I remember those words, "Stay faithful!"

We will never lose if we never give up. Think about the word faithful. When we hear that word we usually think of someone who is consistent, true to his word, and doesn't give excuses. We usually associate faithfulness with someone who has a strong character.

I believe those are all great assumptions, but what creates a faithful person is being full of faith. What is faith? Hebrews 11:1 (NKJV) reads, "Now faith is the substance of things hoped for, the evidence of things not seen."

For a Christian, faith is a belief that God is not limited by our inability to see something with our natural eyes or mind. The person who is faithful is someone who is fully convinced of something he cannot see.

THE PERSON WHO IS FAITHFUL IS SOMEONE WHO IS FULLY CONVINCED OF SOMETHING HE CANNOT SEE.

If you are in need of patience, then you have to remember where your faith lies. Your faith should not be in people, not in a system, nor in education. It's not in a church or in a pastor. *Your faith must be in God.* You are called. God has chosen you. He does have a plan for you, but you have to submit to it and trust in Him. As one Proverb says, "A man's heart plans his way, but the Lord directs his steps." (Proverbs 16:9 NKJV)

Proverbs 3:5-6 (NKJV) confirms, "Trust in the Lord with all your heart, and lean not on your own understanding; in all your ways acknowledge Him, and He shall direct your paths." **Faithfulness is the antidote to impatience.**

TD Jakes, pastor of The Potter's House in Dallas, Texas says, "God directs steps not elevators." Still, we want the elevator. We want to grow, to excel, and push the limits. That makes it hard to obey when God asks us to wait. The generation who grew up in the wilderness wandered in the desert. They watched their parents complain, walk in circles, stuck in a rut. Surely, they could do better, but their time had not yet come.

Those of us who stick it out in the wilderness will see the promise. In our times of waiting, God builds our character. It was in the field that David wrote the Psalms. It was in jail that Joseph interpreted dreams, and it was during 30 years as a carpenter that Jesus was prepared for His ministry.

What is your waiting place? It's possibly working a job that has nothing to do with the career path you desire. Perhaps it's working under somebody that is stuck in a rut, who keeps doing the same things expecting new results. Don't worry, your time is coming. Don't despise the wait.

Rebellion

Finally, we read that Saul was found guilty of rebelling against God, "For rebellion *is as* the sin of witchcraft, and stubbornness *is as* iniquity and idolatry. Because you have rejected the word of the Lord, He also has rejected you from *being* king." 1 Samuel 15:23 (NKJV) Rebellion is as witchcraft!

Witchcraft. This is scary! I have a tendency to rebel, to fight the status quo. I remember my senior year of high school. My grades were excellent, but my school principal threatened to prevent me from graduating because I did not show up for class. I knew the material. School just was not challenging enough. In my head I thought, "Why should I go?" By the way, it's ok to ask why if you are open to God's answer and sometimes His answer is, "Because I said so." Wow! Nobody likes that answer, but the opposite of rebellion is obedience.

How do you defeat rebellion in your life? Easy… obedience. Obedience is the love language of God. Jesus said, "If you love Me you will obey My commandments." (John 14:15)

OBEDIENCE IS THE LOVE LANGUAGE OF GOD.

Out of our love for God, we obey what He asks of us. Does it always make sense to our minuscule minds? Not usually, yet we recognize its rewards. We stay under God's authority when we obey.

Jesus learned this principle well, and it's my personal belief that He learned it from His earthly caretaker, Joseph. We know that Joseph was not Jesus' father, but was given the task of raising Him. If Joseph's life was marked by one word, I would say it was obedience. God told him to marry Mary, to take her to Egypt, and then to Nazareth which fulfilled prophecies about Jesus. Joseph's life was marked by hearing the voice of God and obeying it.

When Jesus prayed before He was about to go to the cross, His flesh said, "Please, God, don't let Me have to do this." But then He said these words, "Nevertheless Your will not Mine." (Luke 22:42)

What a powerful statement! *God, not My will but Yours.* If the Son of God was called to remain under authority, why would we not be expected to do the same?

<u>Pastor's Challenge:</u>

If you recognize rebellion in your heart and if you find it difficult to obey, ask the Holy Spirit to bring the cause of this rebellion to light. Have you experienced a good human example of obedience? Have you observed the blessing of obedience to God? Are you focused more on the promises of God than on your relationship with Him?

I challenge you to walk in obedience. One day Joshua was called to the battle. He saw that it would take a miracle to win a victory, so he prayed an audacious prayer, "God, stand the sun still." (Joshua 10) Steven Furtick published a great book about this moment. God did; and Joshua won the battle, but if he had not been under the right authority this moment would not have happened.

We all have leaders in our lives. Let's honor our leaders and honor the authority God has placed over us. Let's be thankful for them and let's lift up their arms over our lives, even when they are tired and want to give up. That's the way to victory for us.

Chapter 6

POSITIVE ATTITUDE

"If the Lord delights in us, then He will bring us into this land and give it to us, 'a land which flows with milk and honey.' Only do not rebel against the Lord, nor fear the people of the land, for they *are* our bread; their protection has departed from them, and the Lord *is* with us. Do not fear them." (Numbers 14:8-9 NKJV)

Zeal, passion, fervor, energy, excitement, intuitive, vibrant, exuberant, driven, are all great adjectives that describe a young leader God wants to use. But the strategy the enemy wants to use to stifle your drive or hustle, is a **bad or wrong attitude.**

Nothing stops progress in life like a bad attitude. It's like the story of frogs that fell into a deep pit. A group of frogs traveled through the woods, and two of them fell into a deep pit. When the other frogs saw how deep the pit was, they told the two frogs they were as good as dead. The two frogs ignored the comments and tried to jump up out of the pit with all their might. The other frogs kept telling them to stop, that they were as good as dead. Finally, one of the frogs took heed to what the other frogs were saying and gave up. He fell down and died.

The other frog continued to jump as hard as he could. Once again, the crowd of frogs yelled at him to stop the pain and just die. He jumped even harder and finally made it out. When he got out, the other frogs said, "Did you not hear us?" The frog explained to them that he was deaf. He thought they were encouraging him the entire time.

Preparing for promotion is tough and one of the greatest tools in a tough time is a positive attitude. I love what Charles Swindoll says about attitude:

The longer I live, the more I realize the impact of attitude on life. Attitude, to me, is more important than facts. It is more important than the past, than education, than money, than circumstances, than failures, than successes, than what other people think or say or do. It is more important than appearance, giftedness or skill. It will make or break a company... a church… a home. The remarkable thing is we have a choice every day regarding the attitude we will embrace for that day. We cannot change our past... we cannot change the fact that people will act in a certain way. We cannot change the inevitable. The only thing we can do is play on the one string we have, and that is our attitude... I am convinced that life is 10% what happens to me and 90% how I react to it. And so it is with you... we are in charge of our attitudes.

How true is that? Life is 10% of what happens to us and 90% of how we react. When I look back on my life and think of my regrets, I see they were usually caused by a negative attitude I embraced. A negative circumstance does not always have to produce a negative attitude. We are in control of our attitudes.

A NEGATIVE CIRCUMSTANCE DOES NOT ALWAYS HAVE TO PRODUCE A NEGATIVE ATTITUDE.

Joshua and Caleb are great examples of what it means to have a positive attitude. In Numbers 13 and 14, Moses chose 12 men to spy out the land of Canaan. This was the land God promised to the children of Israel. Moses asked them to find out the answer to six questions: how strong are the people, how many people are there, what is the land like, what are the cities like, is there forestland, and what kind of fruit does the land produce? Once they finalized the results, they were to return and report the information to the people.

When they returned, 10 of the 12 spies spoke well of the land, proclaiming it was all that God had promised, acknowledging that it was truly the land of milk and honey.

That meant it was a land of great quality and a land where a person could build a life – the opposite of the wilderness. The wilderness was meant to be traveled through while the Promised Land was meant to be inhabited. Today's wilderness generation needs to know that where we are now is not a place of habitation. This is only a season. God has so much more for us.

Back to the 10 spies. They saw the goodness of the land, but were blinded by the opposition who would have to be defeated for Israel to claim the land. They told Moses and the people the opposition was too strong, the men were too strong, and the cities too fortified. This discouraged the people greatly and they began to complain, "God has left us to die." (Numbers 14:3) The Bible tells us they began to literally weep.

You see, attitude is contagious. Because of the negative attitude of 10 spies, the children of Israel wandered for 40 years after this moment. They had a defeatist attitude. A defeatist is described in the dictionary as one who has accepted failure. Wow, think about that! Are there areas in your life where you have already accepted failure without even trying? You may be reading this and have not overcome a previous failure in your life. You may have made an inner vow that has kept you from ever moving forward from that failure.

An inner vow is when, through a certain set of circumstances, you determine in your heart you will not allow something to happen again. Many of you reading this are being limited by childhood failures that were meant to mold you, but instead they stopped you. To overcome an inner vow, we must pray and ask God to bring healing to a wound we never let heal.

We have all been guilty of accepting defeat at some point when we are faced with impossible situations and we lose faith. The trouble is, once we have lost faith, we have lost. Faith is our weapon! Paul encourages the young leader, Timothy, to "Fight the good fight of faith." (1 Timothy 6:12). Our battle is not with human flesh; it is within. Our fight is to believe. What dreams have you abandoned because you stopped believing? The sad thing is, most of us die before we reach 30 because we stop dreaming. Our attitude makes the difference.

So, what attitude should a young leader have? What should the attitude of the wilderness generation have been? Well, listen to Joshua's response after spying out the land.

> *"If the Lord delights in us, then He will bring us into this land and give it to us, 'a land which flows with milk and honey.' Only do not rebel against the Lord, nor fear the people of the land, for they are our bread; their protection has departed from them, and the Lord is with us. Do not fear them." (Numbers 14:8-9 NKJV)*

This is the attitude of a humble optimist. One definition of an optimist is a person who believes that good ultimately predominates over evil in the world. It's great to be an optimist, but you should be humble. Humility is knowing *who* your *source* is and *why* you have the victory. I have met many positive people who don't know Jesus. Theirs is a false optimism because without Jesus man has no hope for a better future. It is not possible to change for the better in our own efforts. Our faith must be in God who has made us more than conquerors through Christ Jesus. It is He who has given us the promised land.

We should have the attitude of Joshua, and see the opportunity in the opposition. We must not allow ourselves to be blinded by the idea of struggle. Anything worth having we must fight for. I remember the day one of my teachers in college told me, "Lance if it was easy then everybody would do it." The reality is that God is calling us to do things that are not easy for us, but on the other side of that adversity is the promise. Joshua and Caleb saw the same thing as the other spies, they saw the wall of Jericho, they saw the armies, and they saw the fortified cities. 10 spies fell into fear and two stood on faith. Joshua and Caleb saw opportunity while the crowd saw opposition.

ANYTHING WORTH HAVING WE MUST FIGHT FOR.

So, my question is, what do you see for your life? Do you see eminent failure if you take a chance? Do you see empty promises from God because the road looks too hard or do you see a life of victory? Do you see the opportunities are great? Do you see God moving on your behalf to fulfill what He said He was going to do?

Think about David who stood before Goliath and said, "Who is this uncircumcised Philistine who defies the army of God?" Faith is contagious. I would rather have one person of faith with me than 10,000 doubters. Faith sees what others don't... opportunity. *You are one opportunity away from being who God has called you to be.* What opportunities of faith are around you? Are they financial or involving the people in your life? Maybe they're just hurdles you must overcome? Don't let insecurity stifle your creativity and remember, self-doubt and fear are the only things that can keep you from being victorious.

Our job is to wake up each morning with faith, believing in what we cannot see (Hebrews 11). The 12 spies spent forty days spying out the land. Remember the number 40 in the Bible represents a period of testing, a trial. You can't be triumphant until you have gone through a trial. I believe the 40 days Joshua spent spying out the land was a trial from God to see what his attitude would be. What trials are you in right now? Are you passing the test?

Another key aspect of this story is that after Joshua spoke up, the people did not want to hear what he had to say. As described in the next verse, they wanted to stone him. (Numbers 14:10). Wait a second. Somebody tells you God prepared a place for you, He has great plans for you, and you want to stone him? This demonstrates Israel's declining faith at this point.

I have met many people addicted to their pain. They fear being free because they don't know what it's like to believe again. When I begin to speak faith to them, they push back because that means they will no longer be the victim. Perhaps they won't get the attention they like so much or even worse, they will be forgotten. You can't make somebody else have faith or believe in themselves. If God couldn't soften the hearts of the people, then Joshua didn't have a chance.

I don't know about you, but if I had been Joshua, I would have been severely discouraged. He did everything right as a young leader. He followed God. He believed in God but still, the generation above him doubted and criticized. They had given up! **Don't let people who have given up on their dream talk you out of yours.** Some people are so used to being afraid, they don't know what freedom looks like even when it is right in front of them. Just think, how would the story be different if they had taken Joshua's and Caleb's report to heart? For one thing, they wouldn't have had to wander the wilderness 40 years.

On the other hand, we must realize it wasn't Joshua's time to lead. For Joshua, this was a test, a trial. Don't be discouraged when you have the right attitude or the solution. Maybe you see what needs to be changed, but nothing is happening. Perhaps you see your greatness and others don't. It just means your time is not yet. The right thing at the wrong time is the wrong thing. We have to submit to the timing of God. He is the one who determines when a leader rises and falls. Don't try to lead before it's your time. Self-promotion is no promotion. "Therefore humble yourselves

THE RIGHT THING AT THE WRONG TIME IS THE WRONG THING.

under the mighty hand of God, that He may exalt you in due time" (1 Peter 5:6) Submit to God's timing and your time will come.

God has you in his hands. He will complete the work started in you. If you want to be valuable to all of those in your life, begin to walk, speak, and live in faith. Don't let anything be too big for your God. As I write this, there are dreams in my heart that scare me. Writing this book is probably the greatest challenge of my entire ministry thus far, but I have faith. It's not faith in my ability, but faith in what God can do with the ordinary. *God specializes in using the ordinary to do the supernatural.*

What if Joshua permitted this moment to define his life? Where he stood on the promise of God, he could see the victory and taste the goodness of God, but nobody believed in him. I think most of us would have stopped there. We might have allowed bitterness take root. We certainly would have battled offense in our hearts. How many young leaders have stopped right in their tracks because of bitterness and offense?

Just think about how people treated Jesus, the sinless perfect man. They said, "Can anything good come from Nazareth?" (John 1:46)

Don't look for affirmation from others. Look for your affirmation from God. Don't let others who doubt cause you to have a bad attitude. One day, you will reach that promised land. One day, just like Joseph, you will look at those who doubted you, and you will have an opportunity to bless them. The same people who doubted Joshua and Caleb, were the ones who never reached the Promised Land.

Not everyone who starts the journey with you will reach the finish line. On our journey of obedience to God, people will come and people will go. You should follow Jesus' instructions when He told the disciples to shake the dust off their feet if people didn't receive them. Usually, the ones who criticize us the most are those closest to us. Some people will never let you grow up. They will always see you as that little kid, a disappointment, a failure. Don't let that hinder you. People put others in a box to make themselves feel comfortable and to resist any change in their lives.

Attitude is a daily choice; it doesn't just happen once. In Deuteronomy 30, we understand every day we are faced with a choice to choose life or death, blessing or cursing. Many times, how you start your day determines the direction that will follow. I think this story about the elderly carpenter puts things in perspective.

An elderly carpenter was ready to retire. He told his employer of his plans to leave the house-building business and live a more leisurely life with his wife, enjoying his extended family.

He would miss the paycheck, but he needed to retire. They could get by.

The contractor was sorry to see his good worker go and asked if he could build just one more house as a personal favor. The carpenter said yes, but in time it was easy to see his heart was not in his work. He resorted to shoddy workmanship and used inferior materials. It was an unfortunate way to end his career.

When the carpenter finished his work and the builder came to inspect the house, the contractor handed the front-door key to the carpenter. This is your house, he said, my gift to you.

What a shock! What a shame! If he had only known he was building his own house, he would have done it all so differently. Now he had to live in the home he built none too well.

So, it is with us. Many times we build our lives in a distracted way, reacting rather than acting. We are willing to put up less than the best. At important points, we do not give the job our best effort. Then, with shock, we become aware of the situation we created and find we are now living in the house we built. If we had realized, we would have handled it differently.

Think of yourself as the carpenter. Think about your house. Each day you hammer a nail, place a board, or erect a wall. Build wisely. It is the only life you will ever build. Even if you live it for only one day more, that day deserves to be lived graciously and with dignity. Life is a do-it-yourself project. What could say it more clearly? Your life today is the result of your attitudes and choices in the past. Your life tomorrow will be the result of your attitudes and the choices you make today.

YOUR LIFE TOMORROW WILL BE THE RESULT OF YOUR ATTITUDES AND THE CHOICES YOU MAKE TODAY.

Pastor's Challenge:

Stop waiting for somebody to discover you. Stop waiting for a new prophecy or a word to

come. If God has spoken to you and the seed has been planted, water it, nurture it, speak to it, and watch it grow. Faith doesn't make things easy, it makes them possible!

Your faith will open doors no man can shut. Your faith will give you the confidence to walk in your call and faith will be the breeding ground for your dreams.

Who is your faith in? Is it in God who took 2 million slaves and set them free overnight, God who created a universe in six days, God who used a rock to kill a giant, or God who used eleven foolish men to change the world? Perhaps it's God who brought you out of darkness into light and took you out of mediocrity into a life of purpose. If anybody can do it, it is Him.

THE CALL

"Be strong and of good courage, for to this people you shall divide as an inheritance the land which I swore to their fathers to give them. Only be strong and very courageous, that you may observe to do according to all the law which Moses My servant commanded you; do not turn from it to the right hand or to the left, that you may prosper wherever you go. This Book of the Law shall not depart from your mouth, but you shall meditate in it day and night, that you may observe to do according to all that is written in it. For then you will make your way prosperous, and then you will have good success. Have I not commanded you? Be strong and of good courage; do not be afraid, nor be dismayed, for the Lord your God is with you wherever you go." (Joshua 1:6-9 NKJV)

A Call... think about that word for a moment. The most relevant way we can think about it, is relating the many cell phone calls we receive throughout the day – probably more texts than calls now, but you get the point. When somebody calls you, they have a specific purpose for the conversation, even if it is just to chat and catch up on life. I'm one of those people who doesn't like to talk on the phone for long periods of time, mostly because that means I will have to sit still and give my undivided attention. If we are being truthful, most of us like busyness. We like to be moving and active. We associate busyness with accomplishment. I like what Lysa TerKeurst said, "The stress of an overwhelmed schedule will produce an underwhelmed soul."

Rarely do we take the time to sit down and listen to what God is calling us to. Joshua was appointed as the new leader and he took time to listen to God's Call for that season in his life. I want to encourage you by saying, "God is calling you.

He is reaching out to you for this time and season in your life. Take time out and listen to what He has to say."

As we look back at Joshua, we see specific instructions to him. He has just been appointed as the new leader and God gave him directives on how to achieve success. All of us have been called to a specific arena of life. God chose you to glorify Him in all aspects of your life and the reality is, every person's life has a different context. You are the only person that can fulfill the call of God on your life. I believe the call of God goes far beyond just what you are supposed to do; it also encompasses how you are supposed to do it. God not only gives vision, but He gives the instructions on how to accomplish the vision.

The instructions to Joshua were simple yet profound. There were three specific calls to help Joshua fulfill his calling as a leader. The first was to be strong and courageous. God actually said it three times. I don't know about you, but if He told me something three times, I would pay attention. Fear is the great paralyzer of the body of Christ. Fear makes us believe in something that hasn't happened yet.

Second, He called Joshua to speak the word. If you want to know the direction of your life, listen to the words you are speaking. God called Joshua to make sure the Word of God did *not* depart from his mouth.

Third, God called Joshua to uphold and meditate on the Law. The law He was speaking of was the Word of God – in other words, the history of God. You notice He didn't say, "Know the Word of God", rather He said to *uphold* it. He was telling Joshua, it's not enough to know the truth, but he must apply it.

I am excited to dive into these three calls God gives us as leaders. I'm so thankful God gives a blueprint for success. I pray that through these next three chapters, you will open your heart to hear God's heart for your life, and that the Holy Spirit will reveal to you how you can practically apply these truths right where you are.

Chapter 7

BE STRONG AND COURAGEOUS

"Be strong and of good courage" (Joshua 1:6-9 NKJV)

Have you ever been in a place in your life where it seems like there is an overwhelming theme or principle God repeatedly reveals to you? It feels like every TV show or movie you watch God is trying to get your attention, or every time you hear a sermon it appears God frequently reminds and pinpoints an area in your life. God knows how to get our attention, and usually it's through repetition because we don't always get it the first time.

Three times in the first chapter of Joshua, God urged Joshua to be strong and courageous. When God tells you to be strong and courageous, you better know the road ahead of you will be a tough one! We don't like to hear that, do we? We like to hear, "Once you follow God, it is going to be easy going. You are going to get a raise. Everybody is going to like you. Nobody is ever going to hurt you, and life will be a breeze."

The truth is that once you choose to follow God, you become the enemy's target, but an even greater reality is that you will become a threat to the status quo. Following God is a courageous decision. It takes guts. The American church is suffering through an epidemic of countless believers in God, but not many followers. Why do I say this? In my experience, I have met many people who tell me they believe in God. They believe He exists and even say they love Him. But in Matthew 22:34-38 (NKJV) the scripture says, "But when the Pharisees heard that He had silenced the Sadducees, they gathered together. Then one of them, a lawyer, asked *Him* (Jesus) *a question,* testing Him, and saying, "Teacher, which *is* the great commandment in the law? Jesus said to him, 'You shall love the Lord your God with all your heart, with all your soul, and with all your mind.' This is the *first* and great commandment."

If you have grown up in church, this passage must be familiar to you, but let me give some context to these verses. The Old Testament was filled with **613** laws the Jewish faith followed. When laws were broken, a sacrifice was made for the sins of the people so they could remain in right relationship with God. Jesus came to be the ultimate and final sacrifice for our sins so that we are no longer bound by the law. Read Romans 6 for further study.

However, as Jesus began to teach and show the Jewish people He was the Messiah, the Son of God they were looking for, many did not believe because they were bound by the religion of the Old Testament. In this passage, one of their leaders, specifically a lawyer, tried to trap Jesus. He asked a question he didn't think Jesus could answer, "Out of all of the 613 laws what is most important?" Yet Jesus did answer, "You shall love the **LORD** your God with all your heart, with all your soul, and with all your mind." The key word here is, Lord. This is what separates a believer from a follower. Let me ask this question, "Is Jesus the *Lord* of your life?"

What is a Lord? He is the one you surrender to, the one you take orders from, the one who is in control, and the one you are submitted to. It takes courage to make Jesus the Lord of your life because it means you are no longer in control. It means everything you own now belongs to Him. It means that at any moment in time, He could speak to you and you would obey.

The word, courage means strength in the face of pain and grief as well as the ability to do something that frightens you. I don't know where you are in your walk with the Lord right now, but to accomplish God's will, it is going to require courage. It's going to require grit. It's going to require obedience. In other words, it's going to require doing something that frightens you.

I believe the thing that frightens all of us the most is not being in control. Have you ever been in a car with a bad driver? I have to admit, sometimes I am that bad driver, but we are most frightened when we are in a car we cannot control. Ever been riding with someone who is moving at high speed when you suddenly realize at any moment your life may be in danger? It takes trust to ride with another driver. I will never ride with some of my friends because I do not trust them on the road. God is the most trustworthy driver there is. He is the only one worthy to be called Lord. Just ask Carrie Underwood. (Ha-ha.)

I BELIEVE THE THING THAT FRIGHTENS ALL OF US THE MOST IS NOT BEING IN CONTROL.

Joshua had a call on his life. God was giving him the opportunity to make history. What were God's words to him? Be courageous! We need to ask ourselves every day, "Do I have the courage it takes to follow Jesus?" Don't let fear decide your future. Fear paralyzes. I believe there are two fears that keep the wilderness generation paralyzed.

Fear of Man

First, is the *Fear of Man.* Proverbs 29:25 (NKJV) says, "The fear of man brings a snare, but whoever trusts in the Lord shall be safe." In the original text, a snare meant a noose for animals. Think about how a trap is set for animals. My own personal hunting experience is very limited, but I remember setting traps when I was a young boy. Growing up, we had a swimming pool in our back yard and for some reason, every so often the pool and the things around it attracted mice. What do you do when you have mice? You strategically position a trap, place cheese on it, and check it the next day to see if you have snapped the mouse's neck with the trap. Pretty graphic image, right? Well, that's the image this scripture is giving us.

Pause a moment and consider how much time you spend trying to impress people. We live in a society that determines our worth by how many likes, follows and retweets we receive. Social media has become a medium by which we judge our lives. If we don't live up to the highlights of everybody else's life, we feel less than valuable. Our value is not based on popularity or social status, but rather a price that was paid for us. God looked at you and said you are worth His Son. He put a price on you and its worth is immeasurable.

Another reason we don't change is that we are afraid to make people feel uncomfortable. How much time do we spend afraid of how someone might react if we were to change? In this current politically correct season of culture, we are supposed to be tolerant of every person and their lifestyle. Tolerance means to permit something.

When we begin to tolerate the culture around us, we are giving it permission. Jesus did not give permission to sin, in fact He said, "I came that you would sin no more."(John 8:11) When I was a young boy my father would tell me, "Lance, if you don't stand for something you will fall for anything." This is a picture of the wilderness generation as well as the millennials – the wilderness generation of today. Many of us are looking for causes to support without standing for what is true. We should be living our lives on the premise that God is the One who gives the meaning to truth and to life. We have the same mission as Jesus; to seek and save that which is lost. (Luke 19:10) There is no greater cause than seeing people be in relationship with Jesus and know where they will dwell for eternity. I see many millennials support causes that have no eternal impact. If what you are doing with your life does not affect eternity, then you are wasting your time.

IF YOU DON'T STAND FOR SOMETHING YOU WILL FALL FOR ANYTHING

So I ask you this question: is the greatest desire in your life to please God? If your sole desire in life is to please God, then you will never have to worry about what others think about you. This does not make you self-righteous, it makes you dead to self so that Christ can live through you. We, in our own strength, cannot change our culture, our friends or our family. It is through Jesus that people are made aware of His truth. When we trust in Him we avoid the snares of the enemy.

Fear of Failure

Second, is the *Fear of Failure.* This is something I have struggled with myself. The fear of selling out to what God has promised, only to fall on my face, is very real. Then the classic question, 'what if' I'm labeled as a failure by those that I love? What if I disappoint myself?

To deal with this fear we must ask God, "What is failure?" We need to know His answer before we react. Fear of failure is healthy once you realize what true failure is. Failure in God's eyes is *disobedience.*

In Hebrews 11:35-40 (NKJV) we read a description of many prophets' lives,

> *Others were tortured, not accepting deliverance, that they might obtain a better resurrection. Still others had trial of mocking's and scourging, yes, and of chains and imprisonment. They were stoned, they were sawn in two, were tempted, were slain with the sword. They wandered about in sheepskins and goatskins, being destitute, afflicted, tormented—of whom the world was not worthy. They*

wandered in deserts and mountains, in dens and caves of the earth. And all these, having obtained a good testimony through faith, did not receive the promise, God having provided something better for us, that they should not be made perfect apart from us.

Hebrews 11 is the great chapter of *faith heroes.* It commends great men and women of the Bible who, by faith, accomplished great things. At the end of the chapter in verse 32, Paul says he does not have enough time to share all the stories of people who followed God. He then shares in verses 35 – 40, some of these men and women of great faith did not achieve great feats. In the world's eyes, they were failures. Some were beaten, jailed, stoned, cut in half, wandered desolate places, were poor, tormented, or homeless, but in God's eyes their lives were a great testimony. Huh? How is that a great testimony? This is where our attitude has to change. Our testimony is not what we achieve rather, *it's how we obey.*

OUR TESTIMONY IS NOT WHAT WE ACHIEVE RATHER, *IT'S HOW WE OBEY.*

We will be judged one day not for what we achieved, but for our obedience. We have to shake off the world's idea of success. Ideas like; how much money we make, how many friends we have, or how many people follow us must go. To judge your success ask yourself, "How obedient am I?" Courage is obeying God when it doesn't make sense to you; taking the first step even though you can't see the whole staircase. No time or energy is ever wasted being obedient to God. We will have no regrets and we will find the greatest freedom in life when we walk in obedience.

And yet the beauty of God is that even when we are disobedient and fail, He gives us another chance. Failure is not a person, it is an event. We should shake off the failures of the past. David, Paul, Moses, and Peter all failed. God specializes in using people who have failed and He leads them to become successful. Don't let *fear* paralyze you. Just like God said to Joshua three times He is saying to us today,

"Be courageous!" The great Michael Jordan said, "I can accept failure; everyone fails at something. But I can't accept not trying."

A great story in Matthew 25 illustrates fear. A man leaves three servants with talents, one with five talents, one with two talents and the last one with only one talent. Now a talent was weighed at 75 pounds and was equivalent to 6,000 work days or 19 years of pay. Talents are not coins. The first two servants used their talents to double the original investment, so the one who had five now had 10 and the one who had two now had four. But the one who had only one talent was afraid (key word, *afraid*) and he buried the talent, meaning he did not use it but instead, he hid it away.

How many of us, because of the fear of losing what we have, never gain anything? This is the fear of failure. In this story the master comes back to his servants and he blesses the first two servants who were profitable. When he sees the last servant buried the one talent, he takes it away and gives it to the one who had 10. God can't use people who bury their talents. Wow! What's buried in you right now? What dreams have died in you? It's not too late for you to use them. Don't let the fear of failure control your life any longer. I plead with you, don't go to heaven with unused and buried talents.

"So never lose an opportunity of urging a practical beginning, however small, for it is wonderful how often in such matters, the mustard seed germinates and roots itself." - Florence Nightingale

And be strong! When we think about strength, we usually think of Arnold Schwarzenegger's body, with Albert Einstein's mind and Batman's gadgets. Now that's some strength, right? But the truth is, our strength as Christians is in direct proportion to our dependence on Christ. The apostle Paul writes it this way in II Corinthians 12:7-10 (NKJV),

"And lest I should be exalted above measure by the abundance of the revelations, a thorn in the flesh was given to me, a messenger of Satan to buffet me, lest I be exalted above measure. Concerning this thing I pleaded with the Lord three times that it might depart from me. And He said to me, "My grace is sufficient for you, for My strength is

made perfect in weakness. Therefore most gladly I will rather boast in my infirmities, that the power of Christ may rest upon me. Therefore I take pleasure in infirmities, in reproaches, in needs, in persecutions, in distresses, for Christ's sake. For when I am weak, then I am strong."

Paul was one of the strongest men in the Bible. Many times people thought he was dead after being stoned or imprisoned, yet he always prevailed. How was this so? I think he understood the strategy to achieve strength. Nobody knows the exact nature of Paul's thorn in the flesh, but it was obviously something Paul saw as a hindrance to his life. It was keeping him from fulfilling the call of God on his life, but after asking God three times to remove this hindrance, he got the revelation that **weakness is just an opportunity to prove strength.**

I enjoy watching the Olympics. There is something special about men and women from all over the world coming together to attain the title of *Best in the World.* I think TV networks do a really good job of reporting the story behind the story. They research athlete's backgrounds to see where they have come from physically and mentally. This might be why I enjoy the Olympics so much. Most of the athletes have a story about why they started in their sport and what motivated them to be great. Not all of the stories are a horrible physical malady or some disease they amazingly defeated, but at some point, each athlete felt like he or she fell short in life and decided to overcome. One of my favorite stories that is dubbed the "Miracle on Ice" is about the 1980 US men's hockey team who overcame surmountable odds to defeat the heavily favored Russia team. They were smaller, less talented, less experienced, but they realized through their greatest weakness, the team chemistry, they were able to find victory by coming together for a common goal.

So, even though you see weakness, God sees opportunity. Where you fall short, God makes up the difference. Our greatest strength in the Kingdom of God is humility. When you know you cannot accomplish greatness without the help of God and others, you are in a

> **WHERE YOU FALL SHORT, GOD MAKES UP THE DIFFERENCE.**

place to receive the grace of God. Remember, in the original text, grace means unmerited or undeserved favor.

Strength is not having it all together, but it's knowing when to ask for help. Strength is waking up every morning and putting on God's armor. Strength is staying connected to your source and realizing you are just a conduit. Strength is the realization of your human frailty. Weakness is the opposite. Weakness is thinking you have it all together. Weakness is not asking for help, and weakness is not seeing a need for God in your life.

We have a weak generation, a generation that is lost, wandering, searching for the meaning of life. The call of strength and courage the wilderness generation was to have was the courage to obey God's plan for their lives and the strength to realize they could not do it alone. Joshua took the wilderness generation and transformed them into a force of nature. They defeated thirty-one kings and proclaimed the land as theirs. God can take one person with courage and strength and use him to change the course of history.

Don't try to be the leader who has everything. One thing the wilderness generation admires is authentic leadership. They respect leaders who have the courage and strength to say, "I'm not perfect." There are times I'm afraid or I don't have it all figured out, but I will persevere. I will choose obedience and I will follow the Lord into the promised land. Don't be afraid of authenticity. Your greatest anointing will come from it. Remember, the day David danced naked in humility to honor God was a turning point in his life and the statement to his embarrassed wife was, "I will become even more undignified than this." Let your life be marked by the courage you evoke to follow after God.

Pastor's Challenge:

In which areas of your life are you weak? In what area are you depending on your own strength? Where are you allowing fear to paralyze you? I challenge you to trust God with all of your heart and see where he will direct you. "Trust in the Lord with all your heart, and lean not on your own understanding; In all your ways acknowledge Him, And He shall direct your paths." (Proverbs 3:5-6)

If you feel like a failure, remember, failure is not a person, it's an event. God is not through with you. If you have been walking in fear, it's time to wake up out of your slumber and start living. Do you need to deal with pride in your life? Confess it! So that you will be made strong again.

Chapter 8

SPEAK THE WORD

"This Book of the Law shall not depart from your mouth, but you shall meditate in it day and night, that you may observe to do according to all that is written in it. For then you will make your way prosperous, and then you will have good success." (Joshua 1:8 NKJV)

One of the smallest parts of a ship is the rudder. The rudder doesn't determine how fast the ship goes, it doesn't determine the comfort of the ship, it doesn't determine the capacity of the ship, but it does have the most important job because it determines the direction of the ship. In James 3, God tells us that our tongue, even though small, determines the direction of our life.

Let's take a look at these two verses we began with. They could be a book all by themselves. The call to Joshua was that the "law" should not depart from his mouth. As we have talked about previously, the law was the commandments God taught when He told the people how they should live. This was the foundation of their faith. It was the law that was given to them through Moses.

The word, depart in this context means to cease existing. God told Joshua never to let the law *cease existing* in his mouth. Another term for the "law" is God's Word. This was the beginning of the story of God's love for mankind. We know the ending; Jesus came to fulfill this law. The Word of God became flesh and dwelt among us. (John 1:14) God laid out a blueprint that is still relevant in the New Covenant for success. The blueprint is this: The Word of God should always be in our mouth. We must meditate on it always and then do what it says.

Let's take a moment to examine the first step. The Word of God should always be in our mouths. The crux is that if you don't know the Word, then it can't be in your mouth. **The success of today's wilderness generation is dependent on how well we know the Word and our ability to speak it.** Look at this passage in Matthew.

> *Either make the tree good and its fruit good, or else make the tree bad and its fruit bad; for a tree is known by its fruit. Brood of vipers! How can you, being evil, speak good things? For out of the abundance of the heart the mouth speaks. A good man out of the good treasure of his heart brings forth good things, and an evil man out of the evil treasure brings forth evil things. But I say to you that for every idle word men may speak, they will give account of it in the day of judgment. For by your words you will be justified, and by your words you will be condemned. (V.12:33-37 NKJV)*

Jesus is warning us about the power of our words. When our son was four years old, God impressed on Olivia and me to really implant the word of God in our children, so at four years old, our son could quote eleven scriptures. These scriptures became a reference point for him when life came his way. When he was afraid he would quote, "Genesis 26:24. Do not be afraid for I am with you." When something was hard, he quoted, "Philippians 4:13. I can do all things through Christ who strengthens me." When angry he said, "Proverbs 14:29. People of understanding control their anger." You see, the word of God is our greatest tool. It is the only offensive weapon in the Armor of God listed in Ephesians 6. If we are unarmed, we are not dangerous.

If you are married, you can probably relate to this example. There have been times my wife is upset with me because of my "tone." For instance, she might ask, "Hey, Babe, can you clean out the garage? My response might be, "Sure, I would love to." (sarcasm included) Then suddenly I notice she is upset. I can tell when a woman is upset because every time they're asked a question, only one-word answers are the response. Not a good sign.

Finally, when we get to the bottom of what happened, Olivia will let me know she didn't like the way I reacted to her. Inevitably, I defend myself by saying reasonably, "Babe,

I said, sure I would love to." Then she says those words we have all heard before, "It wasn't *what* you said but *how* you said it." Could this be us? Could we be saying the right things, but with the wrong heart? Dr. Albert Mehrabian's studies show that 7% of communication is what you say, 38% is how you say it, and 55% is non-verbal communication.

OUR LIVES HAVE AN ACCENT JUST AS OUR SPEECH DOES

Our lives have an accent just as our speech does. One of the questions I love to ask when I meet people is where they are from. I try to guess from the accent I hear. You know, there are so many accents just around the United States, not to mention around the world. If you hear somebody talking who's from Louisiana and somebody from Texas, the accents sound totally different from each other. It's the same with people from Boston and New York. It's fascinating really. You can hear an accent and it will instantly remind you of something or somewhere else if you've heard it before. Through someone's speech, you can be flooded with certain feelings or emotions. Our lives also have an accent.

What is your accent? Joshua's was the Word of God. I like to put it this way; Joshua branded his life by the Word of God. Nowadays, we have many avenues for our voices to be heard through the internet. Whether you realize it or not, you are creating a brand for your life through what you post on social media. Who you associate with, the blog you write, how you talk to coworkers, how you handle stress, and how you treat your family all influence your brand.

Christianity needs a rebrand in western culture. Companies will rebrand themselves all the time to make sure they are still relevant to the current market. Somewhere along the line, Christians receive a bad rap, so much so that according to a Barna study, only 20% of millennials think attending church is important, and then 35% take an anti-church approach. People don't see the church as important and some even see it as something bad for society. According to Forbes, the number one sign that a company should rebrand is when you are embarrassed to be associated with your company. I believe many Christian millennials are

ONLY 20% OF MILLENNIALS THINK ATTENDING CHURCH IS IMPORTANT

embarrassed by the American Church because we have missed the mark in many ways.

Many Christians have been labeled as hypocritical, judgmental, out of touch with reality, old school, not relevant, and money-hungry. Now we know these stereotypes are unfair and although we identify the failures of Christian men and women in the past, this is not the majority of those who follow Christ. We have to work at fighting these labels and the only way we can do that is by taking a different approach.

Twenty years ago all we had to do to get people to come to church was open our doors. Today, people are not going to come to your church just because you have a building or a space; **they need a reason**. What need is being met in their lives? What would cause them to see a reason to be there?

We must stop having church meetings and start being a church movement. God never intended for the church to be limited by a building, a specific time, or a specific day. God calls the people the church. He desires His Church to bring His Kingdom to Earth. This starts with how we speak, our tone, and our body language. What does our communication have to say about our God?

The truth is, if you want to be successful you have to first speak the Word of God. If you don't know what to say, speak the Word. Jesus said, "What I tell you in the dark speak it in the light." (Matthew 10:27) I believe it can be turned around as well. Whatever Jesus speaks in the light, don't forget it in in the dark. Speak the Word. The Word is the bread of life. It is our source of spiritual nutrition. Paul said, "For I have determined to not know anything among you except Jesus Christ and Him crucified." (1 Corinthians 2:2)

I can spend just a few moments with someone and by what I hear them say, I can determine what type of person they are. What's coming out of your mouth? It's either life or death. It's either the Word of God or it's not. You are either building people up or you are tearing them down. The tongue is a powerful tool that can be used for good or for bad. We lose influence in an instant because our talk doesn't match our walk.

WE LOSE INFLUENCE IN AN INSTANT BECAUSE OUR TALK DOESN'T MATCH OUR WALK.

There are over 7,000 promises in the Bible. That's over 19 promises a day for a whole year. Let's just say you sleep a minimum of five hours a day. That's one promise God has for you every hour of the year.

David wrote in Psalms 139 that if we were to number God's thoughts for you, they would outnumber the grains of sand on the earth. Through some research, we find there are seven quintillion and five hundred quadrillion grains of sand on the earth. If you break that down by 100 years, which is 365 days a year, then 24 hours a day, then 60 minutes in each hour, then 60 seconds in each minute, you will find that every second you live in a 100-year life, God had over 2 billion thoughts towards you. How does a God have over 2 billion thoughts a second for every human being on the planet at the same time? Exactly! It's unfathomable, but when we think about keeping God's Word in our mouth, we need to realize He is always speaking to us. He speaks to us in the quietness of our day and in the hustle and bustle of our weekly routine. **He is always looking to get our attention.** He wants to be involved in every area of our lives.

As we read His promises in the Bible and as we tune into hearing His thoughts toward us, we begin to understand who God is. Once we realize who God is, then we can begin to speak like Him much like we would with a best friend or a family member.

Have you ever had a friend or sibling who could complete your sentences, and you theirs? It's like you could finish each other's stories and thoughts? God wants that same connection with you so you are both speaking and thinking the same thing. Sometimes we think God speaks in the King James Version but that is the furthest thing from the truth. The original text wasn't even written in King James English. It was written in Hebrew and Greek. King James was just the first to translate the book into English.

God speaks to us in a relevant way so we can understand Him. That's why we have many versions of the Bible. He knows how to relate to each of us and to our hearts. When you are keeping God's Word in your mouth, it is not always a verse quoted verbatim from the Bible, and neither is it always eloquent. It just has to have truth as its basis and paraphrase the verse. For example, if I tell my son, "Nothing is impossible for you when you lean on God." Is that a scripture in any Bible? No, but it contains the truth of Scripture.

In many instances when God is speaking to our hearts, we call it our conscience. It may be our conscience talking to us, but God is speaking through it. Here's how I determine whether God is speaking to me or the thoughts are my own. Everything good comes from our heavenly Father (James 1:17) and we know the flesh is wicked. By nature, I am wicked. I am selfish and self-centered. If my thoughts are wicked and selfish, I know it's me. If my thoughts are good, if they connect me to God, if they are thoughts of helping others, and if they are thoughts of joy, they are from God.

Your words are the most creative tool in your possession. When God created the earth, He did it with His mouth. He spoke things into existence. In a dream, God told

Ezekiel to prophesy to dry and dead bones; in other words, to begin to speak the word over them. As he was prophesying, the bones started to come together, the muscles started to form, the skin came upon them but they had no breath. God told Ezekiel to prophesy, and speak the breath of God into them. As Ezekiel opened his mouth, the breath of God filled the bodies.

What's dead in your life right now? What dreams have died? Where have you lost hope? Begin to speak the Word of God over your life. Begin to proclaim His promise and truth and see the miracle of the Lord. You can't have a positive life with negative words.

> **YOU CAN'T HAVE A POSITIVE LIFE WITH NEGATIVE WORDS.**

Joshua would have never reached the Promised Land. He would have never fulfilled his destiny if his words didn't line up with God's. Stop judging yourself so harshly and start seeing what God sees. Don't be your own worst critic. You've got to be your best encourager. When David was faced with an angry mob, the Bible says he went away and encouraged himself in the Lord. He gave himself a pep talk. Sometimes you need to get alone and just start speaking life. Start declaring God's word over you.

One of the darkest times in my life was when Olivia and I were newly married. My income was a mere pittance, I was helping a church plant, and I felt like I was going nowhere. The Lord spoke to me and said, "If you don't believe in yourself, then nobody else will." I realized I was waiting to be "discovered" before I lived my full potential. Don't wait for somebody to discover you. Don't wait for your big break before you start walking out the promise of God in your life. I began to speak my future into existence and things turned around. Don't wallow in self-pity. Speak to the dry bones in your life. Speak the breath of God into them.

"Prick him anywhere; and you will find that his blood is Bibline, the very essence of the Bible flows from him. He cannot speak without quoting a text, for his soul is full of the Word of God." - Charles Spurgeon

Pastor's Challenge:

Take a minute here and consider the inventory of words you are using in your daily life. Are your words lining up with God's Word? What negative words do you need to eliminate?

The wilderness generation of today will never rise to the occasion unless we unlock the potential of the tongue. Your tongue will open up doors, proclaim promises, and guide you into your future. Don't under-estimate its power. Just like anything that has potential, discipline is the tool that sees potential fulfilled.

Chapter 9

MEDITATE AND OBSERVE

"This Book of the Law shall not depart from your mouth, but you shall meditate in it day and night, that you may observe to do according to all that is written in it. For then you will make your way prosperous, and then you will have good success." (Joshua 1:8 NKJV)

Rick Warren says, "If you know how to worry then you know how to meditate." Meditation is often an unfavorable term among evangelicals because of the New Age movement. 20 times, the Bible tells us we should meditate on

God's word. **Healthy meditation is the secret to a healthy thought life.**

The word meditate means to speak or to utter or dwell on. In this particular verse, I believe it's talking about speaking to yourself silently, not speaking out loud because it already mentioned, we are told to keep God's Word in our mouths. I believe God was telling Joshua to continue to speak and utter the Word of God in his heart and mind. Meditating on the right things is healthy for our soul. It keeps us balanced and centered.

Whether you realize it or not, you are always meditating on something. Your mind is always working. You have the choice to decide what you meditate on. The Word of God comes alive in your meditation. When I was in Bible school, we were required to memorize over 400 Bible verses within the first year. This has changed my life. To this day, I meditate on those verses. I am still gaining understanding from God's Word I memorized over 14 years ago.

The call to meditate on the Word of God is the cure for anxiety, depression, fear, doubt, and shame. What we focus on makes a pathway for our feet. When we focus on God's Word, we tend to stop looking at our shortcomings and start seeing God's power at work in our lives. In Isaiah 55:8-9 it says, "God's thoughts are higher than our thoughts and his ways are higher than our ways." When we meditate we connect with God, His thoughts, and His ways.

Why do you suppose God told Joshua to meditate? Up to this point in time, Moses was the sole and only leader of God's people. Moses parted the Red Sea. He witnessed the plagues of Egypt. He saw God speak from a burning bush. He was on the mountain top and heard God speak the ten commands for Israel. Moses was an amazing leader and yet, the people still wandered in the desert for 40 years. Can you imagine the insecurities and fear Joshua experienced? I can envision him saying to himself, "If these people complained while they followed such a great man as Moses, how will they ever follow me? What do I have to offer? What if nobody listens to me? What if I'm the leader responsible for never reaching the land God promised us?"

You see, for every question you have, God has a promise. He knew Joshua had to meditate, continually repeat the promise to himself, and speak the Word of God over his life.

FOR EVERY QUESTION YOU HAVE, GOD HAS A PROMISE.

Meditation will cause faith to rise up and soon we start to believe the promise can come true. Before long, we begin to believe God's Word will not fail us and that He is trustworthy.

Meditation is both for day and night. I have found in my own life, that how I start and finish my day is important. Usually how I end an evening determines how I start the next day. The enemy attacks at all times, but he is especially successful at night. Why? Because we are tired. When we are tired we have one choice to make. Are you going to let God and the Word refresh you or are you going to turn to temporary pleasure? The enemy attacked Jesus in the wilderness after 40 days of fasting, because he knew Jesus was at His weakest then.

Now don't get me wrong. I'm not telling you that you must have a Bible study every night instead of hanging out with friends, family, or watching TV. The last thing that should be on your mind before you nod off to sleep should be the Word of God. It has an uncanny power to rejuvenate and refresh your body, soul, and spirit. I have found when we follow the call of God, we experience many ordinary days, but each ordinary day is filled with supernatural possibilities. Our sensitivity to the Spirit of God can be blunted by the ordinary routine of our days, but mediation keeps us sharp. It's important to see yourself as a room-changer and a culture-setter so that when you show up, a room's atmosphere changes. You bring supernatural wisdom, insight, and energy wherever you go because your spirit has been empowered by your meditation on God's word.

Healthy meditation requires turning down the volume of life so you can hear God. I have found God speaks in the whisper of my heart. In 1 Kings 19, God took Elijah to a mountain and a great wind came, but God was not in the wind. An earthquake hit, but God was not in the earthquake. A fire flared up, but God was not in the fire. Then God whispered to Elijah. God is always speaking, but we have to turn down the volume of everything else before we can hear Him.

"An unschooled man who knows how to meditate upon the Lord has learned far more than the man with the highest education who does not know how to meditate."

- Charles Stanley

In Matthew 6, Jesus tells us to go to a quiet place when we pray. Do you have a quiet place? To conduct a healthy meditation life, we should have a few quiet places. It's the place where you can turn off your cell phone, away from media, and outside noise. It's a place to unwind where you can throw off the pressures of life; a place to come humbly and meet with God.

Once you are in this place, it's key to have a thankful heart. God asks us to enter His gates with thanksgiving and His courts with praise. God cannot resist a thankful heart. Gratitude sets the foundation for revelation. Have a Bible, pen, and paper handy, and perhaps a journal or maybe an electronic device to write down what God speaks to you.

Sometimes you may stay in a moment of meditation for hours, and sometimes only for a few minutes. It's not about the quantity of time, it's about the quality.

One word from God can change your whole situation. Peace about a decision that has to be made might save you millions of dollars. It might keep you from marrying the wrong person. In our deepest meditation of God's Word, we will find the most clarity. His Word is a light unto our path a lamp unto our feet. (Psalms 119:105) I implore you not to make any major decision without meditating on it first. Don't ask your friends, your parents, or even your pastor. Go to God first. Moses was the great example for Joshua in this. He would go into his tent outside the camp and away from the noise to hear the word of God for the people.

ONE WORD FROM GOD CAN CHANGE YOUR WHOLE SITUATION

Not only did God tell Joshua to meditate on the Word, but He told him to observe the law. Another word for observe is obey. Some of us either observe the speed limit or we don't. We view God's Word in the same way. We either observe it or we don't. We either obey and do what it says or we don't. There is no gray area. Jesus told His disciples that the world would know that they were His by how they obeyed. Obedience requires action. How different would our lives look if our obedience matched our knowledge?

It's not enough to meditate on the Word and then to speak it; we must also *act* on it. Talk is cheap. Henry Ford said, "It's better to hear well-done than well said." Have you ever met somebody who was really good at 'talking the talk' and 'looking the look'? Just looking at them you might think, "Wow! They have it all together." Then, as you get to know them better and see their life up close, you realize it was all just a smokescreen. Their actions didn't measure up to their talk at all.

Joshua, in this instance, could easily talk the talk and look the part. He learned to say all he needed to say. On his deathbed, Moses installed Joshua as the new leader. Joshua was the guy who asked God to make the sun stand still during a battle and it did. He was a great warrior, but none of that would matter if he hadn't obeyed God in his daily life.

Our lives speak much louder than our words ever will. You can speak out what you know, but the only thing you can reproduce is who you are. I remember as a young boy I loved basketball. I watched basketball on TV and I played every day I could at the Boys and Girls Club.

Each year when school started, my grandfather took all the kids to Buster Brown shoe store in the mall to buy a pair of shoes for the new school year. I always picked out the new Michael Jordan shoes. Not only did I have the shoes, but I had the socks, the armbands, the hats, and the T-shirts. I had all the gear for basketball. I remember back in the day it was popular to wear multiple pairs of Nike socks that were different styles. Then we lined up all the Nike signs on our calves with three or four pairs of socks. Let me tell you something, I looked the part. I could talk about most players in the NBA at that time, such as Clyde 'the Glyde' Drexler, Hakeem Olajuwon, Kevin Johnson, John Stockton, and so on. You get the point. But there was one thing missing in my life... athleticism. I have CJD, Caucasian Jumping Disorder. I was not a fast runner, but I loved the sport.

I was the kid who was picked for the team and then after a few minutes of playing, my team was disappointed. Later I realized I was better at hitting people in football than I would ever be playing basketball. This is a picture of many Christians today. We dress up for church on Sunday, we know about the Bible, we can even tell you all about David and Goliath, Noah, and the Resurrection, but our lives tell a totally different story.

The first chapter of James puts it like this, "Do not just be a hearer of the word, but rather be a doer. If you are someone who merely hears the Word and does not act on it, you are like the person who looks in the mirror and forgets what he looks like when he walks away." (V. 23 NKJV) This is so true.

I can think of times in my life when I felt the presence of God so strong; times He came alive to me and He spoke to me. Such great moments – it seemed like everything in life stood still for a second and everything began to make sense because God spoke to me. Peace overwhelmed my heart and faith began to rise. But then if I did not act on the Word and continued to live like I wanted, I would forget what the feeling of being in God's presence was like. Before long, I would start to doubt God had even spoken. It seemed more probable I had just had an emotional experience. Other times, I would try to recreate that extraordinary moment because I thought I needed it to survive. When God speaks, it's powerful, but it's not nearly as powerful as when I live out what He has spoken to me.

Think about this for a moment, revelation is not just knowledge, but the *application* of knowledge. For example, think about a biology lab in school. You can talk about dissecting a frog all day, but you will never have the full revelation until you bring that little frog into the classroom and begin to cut it with the scalpel. This is a picture of so many Christians. We talk about great men and women of faith. We hear the scriptures in church on Sunday morning, and we are inspired, but when it comes to our own lives, we

REVELATION IS NOT JUST KNOWLEDGE, BUT THE *APPLICATION* OF KNOWLEDGE.

would rather talk about somebody else's story than live our own.

I'm a big historical movie watcher because the stories inspire me to continue on my journey, but even I can fall into the trap of just being inspired while resisting the move into action. Something that happens when we read the Bible is, we fail to remember that people actually were living this. They did not know the end. Moses did not know that the Red Sea would part. Joshua had no idea the walls of Jericho would fall. David had no idea that the rock would kill Goliath, and Noah had no guarantee that it would rain. It's easy to move into action when we know a guaranteed end. It's tough when we face persecution, difficulty, and resistance to continue moving forward. If your life were a movie, would it inspire anybody?

John the beloved, Jesus' favorite disciple, His BFF (Best Friend Forever), walked with Jesus for three years. John spent so much time with Him. I'm sure he had stories nobody else did. He said that we know God by obeying His commandments. What a statement! What he meant was, it's not enough to know Jesus. It's not enough to just spend time with Jesus, but we must observe what He is telling us to do, and then we will fully know who He is. We can't fully know somebody until we walk a day in their shoes. That's our goal; to walk, talk, and move like Jesus did on this earth so we will be His body on this earth.

Pastor's *Challenge:*

Are you just a hearer of the Word? Do you look and talk the part, but when people get close to you, they are disappointed? You are the greatest beneficiary of a life fully lived in obedience to God. When you walk in obedience, you receive first hand revelation from God. Perhaps you have had some great moments with God, but because you never acted on what He spoke, you have begun to doubt what He said. Don't doubt in the dark what God spoke to you in the light. He is still the same.

I believe the wilderness generation seeks genuine relationships and faith. Your obedience will guarantee you an authentic life that can be used to reach the promised land. Let's not leave people disappointed when they get close to us. Let them see we are the real deal.

THE PROMISE

The promise, I'll admit, is my favorite part of this book because when we make the choice to follow God, we are never left empty handed. God says He rewards those who diligently seek Him. Now, if you are like me, when you get a new book you look at the table of contents to find the chapters that might intrigue you. However, I challenge you to read the first three sections of this book, not just the promise part. You need to fully understand the context of the promise of God, the preparation we must make, and the responsibility it carries in order to fully receive the promise.

The wilderness generation of today understands the unfulfilled promise. We are used to being told something is going to happen only to be disappointed when our expectations are not met. I believe most Millennials are natural pessimists because of broken promises. We have been assured a college degree is not only a great and necessary milestone in our lives, but also, the open door to a great job with great pay and a great sense of fulfillment. Well, we know that's not necessarily true. Education never brings the fulfillment that a purpose does.

Another example is the fact we have seen the promised vows of marriage shattered, so-much-so that the wilderness generation overwhelmingly does not even want to get married for fear of the heartbreak of breaking that same promise. We have been taught that happiness can come from what we obtain only to find out that nothing can fill the void of emptiness in our hearts except a connection with the Creator.

There are two things God cannot do; He cannot lie and He cannot fail. If God has said it, you can believe it. Before you read this next section, please lay aside all the broken promises in your life. Don't put God in a box, and stop dismissing Him by thinking, "Oh, I have heard this before." Remember that God is not your parents, your spouse, your friends, your teachers, your coaches, your boss, or your culture. He is unique and there is no one like Him. He has both the power and the desire to see His promise fulfilled in your life.

There is one major stipulation for receiving the promise of God in your life and that is *submission*. You can only receive the promise of God, if you are submitted to Him and His plan. I think of this submission as my blessing.

Instead of surrendering their lives to God, many Christians bring their own plans to Him. They present God with what they think should happen, how they think it should all play out and then ask God to bless it." Sorry! God does not work like that. There can only be one guide, only one leader, and only one ruler – God. I have heard it said that if you want to make God laugh, tell Him your plans. God's ways are higher than yours and His thoughts are higher than yours. I thank the Lord for that because we would all be in trouble if His thoughts were as limited as mine.

In order to receive the promise of God, we need to submit to the plan of God. We all should let God heal our hearts from broken promises of the past. Let Him restore our faith to believe again. At one time, we all believed with the faith of a child that we could change the world. Let's start to believe again.

In this section I want to discuss the three promises given to Joshua as he led the wilderness generation into the Promised Land. God assured Joshua he would be a pioneer, that he would be unconquerable, and that he would not be alone. I believe today, right now, the Lord is making those same three promises to you and me. He desires that we blaze trails where nobody has been before and that nothing can stand in our way. I believe He is making the greatest promise of all today... that His presence is with you. Man, this gets me pumped to share because it's important we know the reward we get when we diligently seek God. The promise is the reward. The reward is the promise.

Chapter 10

YOU ARE A PIONEER

"Every place that the sole of your foot will tread upon I have given you, as I said to Moses. From the wilderness and this Lebanon as far as the great river, the River Euphrates, all the land of the Hittites, and to the Great Sea toward the going down of the sun, shall be your territory." (Joshua 1:3-4 NKJV)

In 2016, millennials spent over 200 billion dollars in travel. They represented over 70% of all hotel guests. 70% of the millennials who traveled said the meaning of their trip was to explore and experience their destination. According to Millennial Marketing, a company dedicated to educating large companies on how to reach this generation, millennials are labeled as "experience pioneers." This generation values experience over products. This is not an accident. God has put something in us that desires to live life, not just learn about it.

Let's look at the implications of this scripture. God was telling Joshua, and therefore us, that everywhere he goes, God has already given him the victory. Our promise is directly correlated with where we tread or where we walk. Let me say it this way, God has prepared our way for success. When we follow His direction, we are guaranteed to reach our destination. I want to encourage anyone who is not walking in his or her promise to start moving in it today. Start embracing it. As God spoke to Joshua, "I'm telling you just as I told Moses that there is nowhere you can go that I have not given you success. There is nowhere you can go that does not belong to you." (Joshua 1:3-4)

This promise gave Joshua the courage to move forward, to keep moving forward, and to refuse to stop moving forward. The end of Joshua's life is filled with delegating parcels of the Promised Land, the land he pioneered. Moses freed the people from slavery, but through Joshua, God gave the people a future and an inheritance. God desires for us not only to be free, but to leave a legacy for others to follow.

One day you will dispense the places and spaces God has called you to administer, to the next generation. **The trail you are blazing is setting a path for others to follow.**

A pioneer is the first person into a specific area or region. God has called the modern day wilderness generation to be pioneers. He has called us to pioneer geographically and in different arenas and spheres of life for example; music, movies, medicine, humanitarianism, schools, government, technology, science, and art or as Pastor Lynton Turkington calls it the 7 pillars. God is looking for followers to step into every venue in our culture and shine His light.

To accept this promise, a fresh perspective of yourself may be required. It's imperative to see yourself as God sees you. Start believing in the gift, talent and personality He instilled in you. The Holy Spirit is within you, supplying everything you need to be the pioneer God intended you to be. The second greatest commandment is to love others as you love yourself. If you don't love the person God created you to be, then you will never be able to love others the way God appeals you to.

The wilderness generation of today is weary of mediocrity and of just squeaking by. Growth is painful, change is painful, but nothing is as painful as staying somewhere you don't belong. We desire to reach higher and further than the generations before. We want to expand our horizons and achieve what others before us only dreamed about. Moses had the dream in his heart but he knew Joshua was the one to accomplish it. We should be thankful for any Moses God brings into our lives, for they

GROWTH IS PAINFUL, CHANGE IS PAINFUL, BUT NOTHING IS AS PAINFUL AS STAYING SOMEWHERE YOU DON'T BELONG.

are the ones who have paved the way for our success. They are the ones who paid a price we will never fully understand; to give us a shot at fulfilling the dream God placed in their hearts. Our wilderness generation is a fulfillment of promises given to many generations before us. We have to learn to appreciate the past, but not worship it.

In Acts 2, we're given a picture of the "last days"; the days we await the return of Jesus. It states that the young men will have visions and the old men will dream dreams. I believe the young man's dream and the old man's vision are the same. Moses needed Joshua and Joshua needed Moses. Through their common goal, the children of Israel reached the Promised Land. **We can't be intimidated by one another, but rather work cohesively to accomplish the will of God.**

If you are an older man or woman, God has given you dreams – great dreams, and God wants to see those advance through the generations that follow. Once Joshua reached the Promised Land, he began to follow Moses' instructions to allot land to the tribes. This is so powerful, young leader, today's Joshua. *If you ignore those who have gone before you, you won't know what to do with the promise.*

We are not the savior but we *are* a valuable puzzle piece. We are called to fit into the master plan. God wants to progress this generation to their promised land but it won't happen if we do not respect and honor those who sacrificed for us to get there.

You might be wondering what this looks like for you personally. Well, a pioneer is somebody who blazes a trail. I remember in my early childhood playing a game called, Oregon Trail. My friends and I played this on the early Apple computers. Oh, man! We enjoyed this game because at the very beginning we got to choose the names of people who would go with us on our journey to Oregon. As the game progressed, each of us lost some members of our teams as we struggled through the mountains or tried to raft a river. Some members were even lost to sickness. That game was so much fun, but I believe the real reason we enjoyed it so much was because it spoke to a part of our hearts that wanted to be the first one to go somewhere and achieve something new. To be a pioneer, 'to go where no one has gone before!'

Right now the world as we know it is mapped out. We can access Google Earth and view satellite images of pretty much anywhere. The journey we are on may be geographic for some, but for most of us, the journey of pioneering will be filled with using our gifts, talents and personality to create new, witty, and out-of-the-box ways of living.

Corporate America is not attractive to us because so many of us see no purpose in spending nine-to-five in a company that cares little about us as we do something that has no real effect on our culture. We desire to follow a cause and lay down our lives for a purpose. A paycheck is not as attractive as the smile we can put on someone's face because we cared. This is the pioneering heart. There is a deep angst down in our souls that burns with the knowledge that there must be more to life than what we have been told. The wilderness generation may have been born without owning anything, with only knowing manna as food, with only knowing wandering in circles, but they still had hope!

Hope can be a dangerous thing. Hope gives us the ability to have faith so we can act in love. As long as we have hope, then we have a future. Have you lost your hope? Has your disappointment overwhelmed your hope? If it has, then encourage yourself in the Lord. Seek Him and He will restore your hope. Never settle for a life without hope, for it gives you the ability to believe in bigger and higher dreams.

"Man can live about 40 days without food, about three days without water, about eight minutes without air...but only for one second without hope."

- Lloyd Zeigler

Earlier we talked about how unhealthy fear can affect your ability to answer God's call. There is also something called "healthy fear." There is a fear I wake up with every day, a fear that moves me forward, a fear that changed my life, and a fear that puts life in perspective. Proverbs 9:10 says, "Fear of the Lord is the beginning of wisdom." (KJV)

What? We are supposed to fear God? In this context, fear means to *reverence* God. A reverence for God is the beginning of wisdom. Another way to say it is, a fear of what your life would be like if it weren't for God. This fear is where our hope resides. Our hope is in God, not in our own ability but in God's promise. The root of sin is believing that one has no need for God.

THE ROOT OF SIN IS BELIEVING THAT ONE HAS NO NEED FOR GOD.

Remember when Adam and Eve were in the Garden of Eden? How was Eve tempted by Satan? He said, "If you eat of the tree, you will be like God." (Genesis 3:5) In other words, you will have no need for God. This is where sin and disobedience started – a desire, not a need for God. We can say then that for us to be in God's will, we need to be fully dependent on Him, the One who is able to do far beyond what we can think or imagine.

As described in the Bible, the wilderness generation owned nothing. All they had was what they carried, but they held on to a promise that God would make them a nation, that they would be their own people and no longer slaves.

They believed their lives would not be determined by an earthly ruler. What does that mean for us today?

Many of us in our generation are bound, we are slaves to sin, we are slaves to our careers, we are slaves to our families, we are slaves to our friends, we are slaves to materialism, we are slaves to popularity, we are slaves to drugs and alcohol, we are slaves to how many 'likes' we get, we are slaves to our addictions, and we are slaves to others' opinions of us. In short, we have been enslaved and God wants to free us to be our own people. Just remember, we can't own the land and promise God has for each us while we are enslaved to earthly rulers.

Be Hungry

There are three things that will help you be a pioneer. First, you got to be hungry. Yes, I said hungry. Your desire to leave an imprint has got to be greater than your desire for comfort. Are we not a comfort society? I confess, sometimes I think sarcastically how unfortunate I am that I don't have a Lazy Boy recliner like real men should have because my wife says it would not go with the way she decorated our house. I know I am mistreated. Please, pray for me!

Our cars have seat warmers. We can drive up to a store and have pretty much any food we want in a matter of minutes. If we want to learn something, we don't have to go to the library and pick out a book, all we have to do is get on mighty Google. Convenience has become a way of life, so much so, that we can be 45,000 feet above ground and stay connected to anyone in the world who has internet access.

But if you want to be a pioneer, you have to understand something. It's never convenient, and it's not going to work out like you think it will. Obstacles become a way of life, but obstacles are what separate the weak and the strong. When you embrace the challenge you *stay hungry*.

One of the ways I stay hungry is to guard my passion. What I mean is, there are many things that can easily discourage me or take my focus away from my passion, so I have to guard it. As much as possible, I stay away from negative influences or voices in my life. I have to be willing to accept feedback, but I do that with the understanding that everyone does not know what God has placed in me.

Not only do you have to guard your passion, you must feed it! Yes, feed it! You need to motivate yourself, in fact, you need to be your best motivator. Self-motivation is an art, it's something you must learn and practice. Become aware of what pushes your buttons.

Something that motivates me is thinking about my kids. What legacy will I leave for them? What will they see me do that they will follow? The single greatest legacy I can give my kids is obedience to God. They will see me face obstacles, and see how I respond.

Music is another great motivator for me. What I am listening to can literally determine my whole mood. To sum up, guard and feed your passion so you can stay hungry. God will meet you at the point of your hunger and expectation. He has chosen to be limited by our free will. You can't hunger for greatness while your

GOD WILL MEET YOU AT THE POINT OF YOUR HUNGER AND EXPECTATION.

appetite is content with mediocrity. Mediocrity is the enemy of great pioneers. God will meet you at your expectation.

When you are hungry, it's important to understand the goal is progression, not perfection. Don't get disappointed because you have not arrived, but be thankful you are not where you were. Success is a process, not an event. God gives opportunities but we must seize the opportunity. He cannot do it for us. God has called you to a "land", an arena of life and it's not going to just be given to you. Joshua persistently fought for the promise land.

<u>Use what is in your hand</u>

Second, you have to use what is in your hand. Moses parted the Red Sea with what he had in his hand at the time...his staff. Stop waiting for the perfect circumstance to start being a pioneer. Many of us would be more adventurous if we had things like, more money, more time, more influential friends, a better location, more education, more mentors…the list can go on endlessly. But the truth is, you have to step-out with what you have. Remember Joshua. He had nothing and he owned nothing. He was surrounded by a generation of men and women who never fought before, they had never plowed land before, and were not much more than grown babies, yet God used them to create a nation. God does not call the equipped, *He equips the called.*

As you start to step out with what you have, God will begin to fill every need in your life. There was one point in my life where I was working a secular job and working for a church. After two years, the Lord spoke to me and my wife about searching out full-time employment in a church. We felt like, "Lord, who is going to hire us? What do we have to offer?" And He answered, "You have everything you need right now to fulfill the calling of God."

So, I started to write a resume. At that time, I had very little experience. The resume looked pathetic. I remember thinking, "How can I word this to make myself sound really important?" Yep, it still did not look that great. But I had great faith, so my wife and I began to talk about what our dream job would be. Long story short, after a few months of sending out pathetic resumes we were offered a job. Amazing, right? We quit our jobs and started to get ready to take a new position in a new state. Then, at the last minute the church called and took back their offer with no explanation whatsoever. We faced an obstacle!

We felt like God left us. Have you ever felt that way? Even though we were compromising some things, we felt like everything was working out like we wanted and then, *whoosh*, the rug was pulled out from under us. I remember calling my former employer to ask if I could work a couple of weeks just to pay my rent. I knew I couldn't go return full-time since my position had already been filled. It seemed like we did everything we knew to do to follow the Lord but were left dismayed and disappointed.

Little did we know God had better plans. Within that same week, we were offered another job and it was not just any job. It matched the criteria exactly that my wife and I had talked about when we were planning our dream job. The Lord prepared the way, I just had to be confident in His Word. He had given us everything we needed to succeed and to transition into our calling, but we had to take the first step. Remember, a closed door is direction not rejection. As you take steps some doors will open and others will close, but it is God preparing the path.

God can't trust you with the abundance of the promised land if you are not faithful with the little you have now. TD Jakes tells a story of when he was leading a small Bible study and nobody knew his name. He wrote a sermon every day because he knew one day he wouldn't have the same time he did during that season to study. Are you preparing for your abundance? Use your current situation to your advantage. Don't look at your lack, look at the possibilities.

Jump

Lastly, you have to jump. Yes, jump! Every great movement starts with one person willing to take the leap of faith. You were not made to be stagnant, you were made to propel forward. Sometimes the hardest thing to do is start. The first step is often as simple as beginning to speak your dream. We were made to explore, to test the potential inside us, to traverse whatever hardships may come our way... we are pioneers. Zechariah said, "Do not despise these small beginnings, for the Lord rejoices to see the work begin." (4:10 NLT)

The word, despise means to hold as insignificant. Our beginnings are significant. They are important because how we begin determines the momentum we will sustain to continue. Don't be afraid to start small. The beauty of it all is that the Lord rejoices when you start.

Does that seem different? Most people celebrate after the race is over not when it begins, don't they? We don't celebrate people in life just for trying, do we? Since this isn't the Lord's way of giving out participation awards, we need to recognize something about Him. He is the a*uthor* and the *finisher* of our faith. He sees the end from the beginning. He knows from the moment we launch how we will land and He rejoices when we take the first step. I love this quote from Jon Acuff, "You have to be brutally realistic about your present circumstances and wildly unrealistic about your future circumstances." You have to understand your life will never move forward unless you start, but once you do there are no limits.

In Joshua 3, God called Joshua to cross over the Jordan and promised that as Moses parted the Red Sea, God, would part the Jordan River. Now if you are Joshua you might think, "I'm going to raise my staff just like I saw Moses" and part the Jordan River, but Joshua knew God would move in a different way to walk Israel into the promise. God actually gave Joshua the plan. He was to gather 12 men, one from each tribe, to carry the Ark of the Covenant into the river. Once they stepped into the river, it would begin to part.

The Ark of the Covenant is the representation of the presence of God. Where God leads He provides, but Israel had to take the first step. God cannot take the first step for us, we have to do that, and we carry His presence. The promise was being fulfilled, "Wherever your footsteps I have given you." (Joshua 1:3-4) Nobody walked on dry land across the Jordan before them. What is your first step? Although you have always been afraid to, maybe it's time to pursue the career tugging your heart. Maybe there is a ministry God has placed in you and maybe He is telling you to move. You have to jump! Nobody is going to do it for you. Nobody is going to push you off the ledge. If you want to achieve something nobody has done before, then you have to be willing to live like nobody has before. As I'm writing, I can feel God through the words of this book awakening the pioneer in you. Trust God's voice inside your heart. If you have a God-given dream, then God has already made the way.

Pastor's Challenge:

Do you sense the deep down desire in your soul to be a pioneer? Has your imagination had a chance to run wild and believe the impossible? Are you hungry for change? Has your appetite for greatness been stifled by settling for mediocrity? Do you believe everything you need is already in your hand, and do you have the courage to jump?

"The world is eagerly waiting for the sons of God to be revealed." (Romans 8:19) People around you are looking for leaders who will say, "I don't care who goes with me. I am filled with God-given creativity and I will pursue all God has placed in my heart to do." If you can truly grasp the promise *that everywhere your foot treads, everywhere you walk, God has given you victory*, then you will know He surely has set you up for success.

Chapter 11

YOU ARE UNCONQUERABLE

"No man shall *be able to* stand before you all the days of your life." (Joshua 1:5 NKJV)

William Earnest Henley is known for his popular poem "Invictus." William had an impoverished childhood and battled tuberculosis. One of his legs was amputated and the other leg was saved through many surgeries. In his recovery, he wrote this poem:

You are Unconquerable

Out of the night that covers me,
Black as the pit from pole to pole,
I thank whatever gods may be
For my unconquerable soul.

In the fell clutch of circumstance
I have not winced nor cried aloud.
Under the bludgeoning of chance
My head is bloody, but unbowed.

Beyond this place of wrath and tears
Looms but the Horror of the shade,
And yet the menace of the years
Finds, and shall find me, unafraid.

It matters not how strait the gate.
How charged with punishments the scroll,
I am the master of my fate:
I am the captain of my soul

Invictus in Latin means unconquerable or undefeated. It is said that Nelson Mandela would quote this to the other prisoners to encourage them to keep hope while they were being marginalized. This poem is a reminder that an unconquerable soul is strengthened by insurmountable circumstances. You are unconquerable. You are unbeatable. We know how the story ends and we win.

THIS POEM IS A REMINDER THAT AN UNCONQUERABLE SOUL IS STRENGTHENED BY INSURMOUNTABLE CIRCUMSTANCES.

See, once we make the decision to be a pioneer, we come to believe God has given us the area He is calling us to. However, dominion is not the only thing He promises us. He is also promises nobody will be able to stop us. Conflict is part of the promise. This is where the modern day wilderness generation has failed to mature. Too many of us believe the lie that we are owed something without having to sacrifice for it. If you are afraid of sweat and hard work, then this book is not for you. If you are allergic to sacrifice, long hours, obstacles, bumps in the road, and opposition, then you can't expect to partake in the beauty of winning. Joshua empowered a group of people, who never fought a battle a single day in their lives, to conquer 31 kings.

Our past failures don't define our future successes. Our lack of experience does not disqualify us from Godly wisdom. We have the promise of God that no man can stand against us. There is no person who can stand between you and your God-given destiny, even though the enemy might try to use every means possible to stop you.

Joshua lost one battle, that's it, just one. You can find the full story in Joshua 7. In a nutshell, the people of Israel were commanded not to take any of the accursed items in Jericho since they were meant for the Lord. Without Joshua's knowledge, Achan seized some of the spoils of war from Jericho.

In preparation for the next battle against Ai, the Lord told Israel to send a small army, but as the small army of 3,000 attacked Ai, they were overrun and Israel ran for their lives. Joshua then began to doubt the Word of the Lord. He prayed in anguish, asking why God had forsaken him. The Lord's reply was that there was sin in the camp, and He shared with Joshua that someone disobeyed the command. Joshua then removed Achan and his family and killed them. From then on, the Israelites never lost another battle.

This is a great picture of what disobedience does in our lives. Scholars say that in the wilderness, there were about 2.5 million people, so the disobedience of one had the potential to cause destruction of 2.5 million. I believe this is a picture of you and me. When we are disobedient, we cannot expect to live victoriously.

WHEN WE ARE DISOBEDIENT, WE CANNOT EXPECT TO LIVE VICTORIOUSLY.

God majors in the minor details of our lives. **Details will determine your destiny.** You have to realize nothing is small in God's eyes when it comes to obedience. How do we treat disobedience? We have to kill it. We have to utterly destroy it. We cannot allow space or excuses for it. Jesus said that if your eye causes you to sin, pluck it out (Matthew 5:29) – not literally, but you do have authority to take over your own life and kill the flesh when it disobeys God.

For the modern day wilderness generation, I believe this is really important. We have been caught up in a grace message that proclaims God will always forgive you, so don't worry. The reality is, God will always forgive repentance, but He cannot control the consequences of a sinful life. God's grace empowers us *not* to sin. He guides us to live a victorious life, He does not give us a license to sin. As we have discussed earlier, the word *sin* means missing the mark. It doesn't mean God sees us as despicable or deplorable, rather He sees us as disobedient children who refuse to walk in His will. We cannot please God and please our flesh at the same time.

I believe there are some Joshuas in this generation who say, "I don't want to operate in the gray areas of Christianity. I want to fully surrender and submit my life to the Lord."

As Paul said, "Follow me as I follow Christ." (1 Corinthians 11:1) Paul willingly stopped doing things in his life that would cause others to stumble. When is the last time you declared, "I'm going to be obedient to the call of God and live a life that is not a stumbling block for someone else"? We are not given a choice about which lifestyle we want to live or how much we can handle. Our only real choice is, will we consider and be obedient to the standard God is calling us to? Obedience is the love language of God. We are the ones responsible for our own demise.

Once you have killed disobedience in your life, it's time to dream big. Small dreams and small living are an abomination to the Lord. God's plan for your life is never small. It's never insignificant. It's never menial. He wants you to achieve far more than you can think or imagine.

SMALL DREAMS AND SMALL LIVING ARE AN ABOMINATION TO THE LORD.

You are Unconquerable

"A great leader's courage to fulfill his vision comes from passion, not position."

- John Maxwell

There are some key things to sustaining an unconquerable spirit. You need to remember who called you. God called you. You were His idea. This dream was His idea. God wants you to succeed more than you want to. 1 Thessalonians 5:24 (NKJV) 24, "He who calls you *is* faithful, who also will do *it.*" Start planning like you can't fail. Sometimes when we start to dream, we look for holes in the dream and start tearing it apart. We think of everything that could go wrong. God is on your side. If you could do it on your own, it wouldn't be God. You are going to need all the help you can get.

You also need to create monuments to God along the way. After Joshua crossed the Jordan River, he created a monument to God.

Joshua 4:4-7 (NKJV)

Then Joshua called the twelve men whom he had appointed from the children of Israel, one man from every tribe; and Joshua said to them: Cross over before the ark of the Lord your God into the midst of the Jordan, and each one of you take up a stone on his shoulder, according to the number of the tribes of the children of Israel, that this may be a sign among you when your children ask in time to come, saying, 'What do these stones mean to you?' Then you shall answer them that the waters of the Jordan were cut off before the ark of the covenant of the Lord; when it crossed over the Jordan, the waters of the Jordan were cut off. And these stones shall be for a memorial to the children of Israel forever.

Joshua was setting up a place for the next generations to remember what God had done. This is so important because **He was showing the people this victory was just not His alone, but that the victory was for everyone.** Share your success with those around you. Don't have a, *me* mentality. To get where you are going, you will need a team of people around you. Celebrate with your team. Share your success. The promised land is not just for one generation. Over an estimated 3400 years later, Israel is still benefiting from the obedience of Joshua. What places in your life are you building as monuments to God? Where will you be able to take your children back to and say, "This is where God performed a miracle on our behalf"?

Don't forget the mentors in your life and don't forget the people who saw potential in you. Joshua's success was a result of good mentorship. There are 52 instances where Moses is mentioned in the book of Joshua. Though he may not have seen the Promised Land, though he may not have defeated the kings, though he may not have ever tasted the good of the land, Moses was just as much a part of the victory as Joshua.

Today we have a generation that protests and exercises the freedom of speech on a daily basis more than any other generation before. But what many of these young people fail to realize is, the sacrifice of countless American lives to give them that freedom and what Americans stood for. The principles and freedom of Americans were formed by the principles and devotion to God. We have seen the demoralization of a culture through dismissing those who built the freedoms we enjoy on a daily basis.

Joshua never forgot the dream God put in Moses and he made sure nobody else forgot as well.

"The best way to honor past accomplishments is by building on top of their breakthroughs"

- Bill Johnson

An unconquerable soul builds loyalty to the Lordship of Christ, not to a leader. Loyalty to a leader is shallow and can cause dysfunction, but loyalty to Christ will cause those who follow to be healthy and fulfilled. Joshua never demanded loyalty, but rather, faithfulness to the God who called him. Don't create followers who are more loyal to you than they are to God. When Joshua delegated the land, he was able to appoint leaders and tribes to certain areas and fully trusted their capacity to lead because they were devoted to the Lord.

Lastly and most importantly, we are unconquerable because of Jesus Christ. Let's take a look at this powerful passage that shows us that we are "more than conquerors."

Romans 8:35-39 New King James Version (NKJV)

Who shall separate us from the love of Christ? Shall tribulation, or distress, or persecution, or famine, or nakedness, or peril, or sword? As it is written: For Your sake we are killed all day long;
We are accounted as sheep for the slaughter.

Yet in all these things we are more than conquerors through Him who loved us. For I am persuaded that neither death nor life, nor angels nor principalities nor powers, nor things present nor things to come, nor height nor depth, nor any other created thing, shall be able to separate us from the love of God which is in Christ Jesus our Lord.

The greatest victory we have as Christians is when Jesus Christ beat death, hell, and the grave. When we understand the power of God's perfect love, we will truly be victorious. It was love that held Jesus to that cross, it was love that sent Jesus to this earth, it was love that brought Him out of that grave, and it is because of God's love we are even where we are right now. You see, when Jesus emerged from that grave, He took all the devil had and rose victorious. The devil has been defeated for eternity and he has no more authority on this earth. Jesus restored what Adam forfeited.

JESUS RESTORED WHAT ADAM FORFEITED.

Paul shows us in this passage that we will face problems, hard times, people not liking us, lack, loneliness, or even physical harm, but we will be more than victorious. We not only win, but we win by a large margin. It's like a high school team playing against the NBA All-Stars. God sets us up to win through His Son, Jesus Christ and if we even just resist the devil, he has to flee. (James 4:7)

You might be asking the question, "I know I'm supposed to be unconquerable, but why do I feel defeated?" Well, you have need to understand the only way the devil can attack you. The devil can attack you four different ways: through lies, confusion, your past, and fleshly desires.

Our enemy is a liar

Our enemy is the father of all lies. (John 8:44) What lies are you believing today? If you are believing anything that is contrary to God's word which we know is the truth, then you have fallen into the devil's deception. He will try to convince you that you are not good enough, that God doesn't love you, that you will never make it, that you can't get through the storm you are in, that nobody cares about you… He knows exactly what buttons to push. If you don't know what the Bible says about you, then you will fall into these lies. Once you start believing a lie of the enemy, you are deceived and you will begin to lose your God identity.

Our enemy is the author of confusion

Our enemy is the author of confusion. 1 Corinthians 14:33 says that God is not the author of confusion, so if it's not from God, then it's from the devil. When God speaks, it's clear and concise, but once He does speak, the devil tries to bring doubt, division, and confusion. This speaks to a lot of Christians today who are confused about what to stand up for.

God makes it clear to stand up for truth in the name of love. But we can become confused and may believe that if we disagree or hurt someone's feelings, then we are not acting Christ-like. It's confusion. Also, many of us are confused about our call from God. Let me tell you something. God won't give you the big picture but He will give you the next step. Don't worry about how it all will happen, just take the next step. The enemy wants to paralyze you with worry, anxiety, and inconsequential efforts to determine your life.

Our enemy is the accuser of the brethren

Our enemy is the accuser of the brethren. (Revelation 12:10) To accuse somebody is to say they have done something wrong. The devil knows how to point out every wrong thing you have ever done in your life, but we have to understand Jesus took our place.

2 Corinthians 5:21New King James Version (NKJV)

"For He made Him who knew no sin to be sin for us, that we might become the righteousness of God in Him."

This will preach right here. Jesus who was perfect, who had never sinned, became OUR sin, so that we could be in right standing before God. That means your past no longer has a hold on your future or on your relationship with God. Our enemy is the constant accuser. He is always reminding us, condemning us, and pointing the finger at us. But God has already made a provision for our shortcomings. The devil knows your name but calls you by your sin. God knows your sin and calls you by your name. The devil doesn't know your future so he uses your past.

Our enemy attacks our fleshly desires

Our enemy attacks our fleshly desires. In Matthew 4, Jesus is tempted in the wilderness. Can you relate? The devil came to attack Jesus at His weakest point; when He had fasted 40 days. The devil tempts when you are the weakest, when you are tired, irritated, hurt, hungry… I believe this generation is the most tempted generation in American Culture. Subjective morality is one of our greatest temptations, where we begin to justify our fleshly desires in the name of being balanced. When you are fulfilling desires of your flesh, you will be stuck wandering in the wilderness. The children of Israel were stuck complaining for 40 years. What temptation has your attention?

Clarity occurs when you begin to understand the strategy of the enemy. Just like God uses people to fulfil His purpose, the enemy does the same thing. That's why we need to hold onto this promise, "No man shall *be able to* stand before you all the days of your life." (Joshua 1:5 NKJV). No man nor devil can stand between you and your promise when you don't listen to the lie of the enemy, when you don't fall into the trap of confusion, when you understand Jesus took our place and redeemed our past, and when you choose to feed your spirit instead of flesh.

Pastor's Challenge:

I encourage you to pause right now and examine any disobedience in your life. No matter how big or how small the command you have chosen to ignore, first ask yourself, "What was my motive for refusing to follow this command?" Was it fear, discomfort, or selfishness that paralyzed you? Once you have searched your heart, ask God's forgiveness and then repent.

Repent means to make a 180 degree turn, to go in the other direction. Obey whatever the Lord is telling you to do. Start right this moment. Maybe you need to take a moment and write out a plan of action to accomplish the command of the Lord. Maybe it's breaking off an unhealthy relationship or setting aside an addiction. May it's slowing your schedule down so you can make time for the Lord, or perhaps it's forgiving somebody who hurt you. Whatever it is, begin to move. Obedience requires action.

Once you take the first step, think about these promises God has given you. You can do all things through Him who strengthens you. You are more than a conqueror through Christ Jesus. Greater is He that is in you than he that is in the world. God has plans for you, not to harm you but to give you a future and a hope. No weapon formed against you shall prosper. God is faithful to complete the work He started in you. If you lack any wisdom, just ask God who gives it freely. These are promises for an unconquerable soul.

> GOD IS FAITHFUL TO COMPLETE THE WORK HE STARTED IN YOU.

Now prepare for battle. You have an enemy you will confront. God is going to use you to defeat the enemy that seeks to divide us by our race and ethnicity. God fills our hearts with true love and acceptance that only comes from

Him. God wants to give you insight to open the eyes of a culture insistent on relative truth by exposing good and evil. God's going to give you a boldness to evangelize your sphere of influence for His kingdom. God wants to use you to break the spirit of religion off of the self-righteous. God is going to give you the ability to destroy the greed of American society so we will value people more than money or things. He is going to give you supernatural wisdom about how to defeat worldwide crisis.

Do you believe it? God wants to see us fight for the injustices in our society. Are you starting to see the things on God's heart? The list could go on. But what is God placing on your heart? What cultural enemies has God called you to defeat? Remember, you are unconquerable! **We don't fight for victory, we fight from victory.** Joshua understood this. The promise precedes the victory. When you walk in confidence, no one will be able to get in your way.

Joshua knew he wasn't just fighting the kings in that area, rather, the devil himself. Don't put a face on your enemy. Too quickly as Christians, we start to label people as our enemy but the Word says, "Four our struggle is not against flesh and blood, but against the rulers, against the authorities, against the powers of this dark world and against the spiritual forces of evil in the heavenly realms." (Ephesians 6:12)

So, what's your fight? If you don't know what you are called to or if you are questioning what you are passionate about, then let me help you. What irritates you? What gets under your skin? What are your pet peeves? In those things you can find your calling.

There are a couple of things that really irritate my wife; lack of organization and people who are disingenuous. If you want to upset her then be disorganized and try to be somebody you're not. Through the years as she has committed these irritations to God, I've watched Him use her ideas and attention to detail to change the way organizations operate. I have seen her transform millennials' lives by teaching the characteristics of being trustworthy and less self-absorbed. She has used her complaint as a tool to change the world and she continues to do so.

Nine times in Joshua we see the phrase, "The Lord delivered them into your hand." Joshua fought, but God delivered. The point I'm trying to make is, the fight you are facing right now is the one God wants you to win. All of us fight something, and you need stop asking why you have to fight opponents and instead, start winning the battle.

Joshua knew what whining caused: 40 years of wandering. We need to stop complaining about our problems and start coming up with resolutions. Wouldn't it be nice if God just gave the land to Joshua without one battle and without enduring the longest day ever recorded so he could win? God doesn't work like that. When we pursue the promise, we are given a chance to persevere.

Our trials don't define us, neither does who we defeat. The God inside us defines us. When people see us they will see Jesus. Joshua is a picture of Jesus in the Old Testament. Their names have the same meaning...God is salvation. You, as well, represent the salvation of God wherever you go. **Faithful is the One who has called you and He will do it!**

Chapter 12

YOU ARE NOT ALONE

"Have I not commanded you? Be strong and of good courage; do not be afraid, nor be dismayed, for the Lord your God *is* with you wherever you go." (Joshua 1:9 NKJV)

To be a leader is to be lonely at times. Not everyone is going to understand the call on your life, not everyone is going to see the potential of your life, and not everyone is going to go on the journey with you. John Maxwell expresses it well: "A leader sees things before others see them, they feel things before others feel them, they move before others move, and they see realize that not everybody will make the journey with you"

Before Joshua was going to ever see the promise fulfilled in his life, he had to be aware of one thing. God was with him. No matter where you are at in your journey, it's vital you know God is with you. Why do we need to know this? Well, if God wants us to know He is with us, then we can infer there will be times we will feel alone.

Joshua was the sole leader of the children of Israel. He carried a burden nobody else could understand. He had a plan at times nobody else knew, and he had to make decisions nobody else had to make. Have you been there? No matter how much we try to sympathize with others, we will never truly know what it's like to walk in their shoes

We make this mistake many times when we assume what others are going through. I will never be able to comprehend the weight of what you are carrying right now. I won't be able to fully understand your perspective or prerogative on life, but I do know who can.

This is what separates Christianity from every other religion. We have a relationship with the living God. Not only is He alive, but He has chosen to dwell among us. To me, this is the greatest promise of all. To put it best, look at this mathematical equation. **Nothing + Jesus = Everything.** As long as we have Him, it's enough. His presence is the ultimate promise.

One word from God is greater than a thousand sermons. Many Christians are living off of the revelation that their parents, pastor, or mentors had, and that's great, but it will only last for a moment. When you have a personal revelation of God that is facilitated through a relationship with Him, it will last forever. God will speak a word in season to you directly and it will be the guiding voice that leads you to the next season.

Joshua was about to pioneer one of the greatest stories ever, knowing that nothing would be able to stop him. What's most important, was that God would always be with him. God knew something Joshua may not have known. He knew that if Joshua was lonely, he would not fulfill the call on his life.

HE KNEW THAT IF JOSHUA WAS LONELY, HE WOULD NOT FULFILL THE CALL ON HIS LIFE.

Loneliness is the silent killer of leadership. When we are lonely and not aware of God's presence, we lose sight of our purpose and dreams. Being alone is the world's second greatest fear next to death. We are afraid of being alone. Being alone has nothing to do with not being around people, rather it has to do with people truly knowing who they are.

Have you ever felt invisible, like your life has no meaning or doesn't matter? This is the tool of the enemy. His malicious intent is to make you feel insignificant, that your life has no purpose, and no ultimate meaning. My life verse is John 15:16 (NKJV), "You did not choose Me, but I chose you and appointed you that you should go and bear fruit and that your fruit should remain, that whatever you ask the Father in My name He may give you."

If you really think about it, we have all faced rejection at some point and that rejection has altered the way we view ourselves and how we embrace life. Rejection is the enemy's tool to stifle our self-confidence. Rejection has the potential to lead to depression. I have met more depressed individuals in this generation than I can even count. We have come to believe the lie that if others don't accept us, then there is something wrong with us.

The reality is, Jesus said that if they reject Him, they WILL reject us as well. People reject what they don't understand and what brings discomfort to them. This is why I love this verse. I can be misunderstood, rejected, and overlooked, but God has chosen me. If God has chosen me, it doesn't matter if anybody else chooses me. If God has selected me, picked me, preferred me, then that's all I need.

A deep-rooted issue of why we deal with rejection is fatherlessness. According to 72.2% of the U.S. population, fatherlessness is the most poignant social problem we have. A father is present to love, care and protect, and when a child doesn't know their father, or the father does not know his role, his covering and security is absent. A Generation is trying to prove themselves, trying to find their own path, and trying to find out who they are because a father never told them. If you can relate, I challenge you to look to your heavenly Father to give you your identity and purpose. **He has chosen you! He said you are worth His Son and He wouldn't change one thing about you. Don't correlate your earthly father's rejection to God rejecting you. He is the perfect dad.**

God hasn't only chosen us, but He appointed us. God not only said, "I like you", but He gave us power and position here on this earth as sons and daughters. Your greatest title in life is not your job title, it's not your last name, it's not your occupation, and it's not your degree. It's that you are a son or daughter of the King. You have rights, you have privileges, and you have authority. You have been appointed, ordained, and empowered to walk in the fullness of God's promise.

> YOUR GREATEST TITLE IN LIFE IS SON OR DAUGHTER OF THE KING

If you are facing rejection right now, maybe from those who are closest to you, remember God has not forgotten you. You are loved, you are cherished, and God still has a plan for your life. Rejection is, often times, direction. Remember, Jesus told us we would be rejected. Don't let bitterness take root in your life. If you feel misunderstood, don't shy away from the dream God has placed in your heart. In due time, others will see the same potential God sees.

Some of the loneliest people can seem to be outgoing extroverts, but inside they feel as though nobody cares about them. Being a leader can be lonely since you have been chosen by God to stand out. You might have some Friday nights by yourself and you may not get invited to all the same events or parties as other people. Because of your standards, people may mistreat or judge you. It's a part of the call to leadership. But the promise of leadership outweighs the call. **GOD IS WITH YOU!**

Joshua saw his leader, Moses, emphasize the presence of God. Moses was faced with one of the most difficult choices. In Exodus 33, God tells Moses that Israel can go into the Promised Land, but He will not go with them because of their whining and complaining. Moses' response is, "God, if You will not go with us then I do not want the Promise Land."

Wow, so amazing! What if God just said to you, "You can have everything I have promised you right now, but there is a catch. You may never hear My voice or be aware of My existence again"? What a hard choice; to choose to suffer in God's presence or promise without His presence. What Moses understood was that God's presence was the greatest promise of all. After all, it was God's voice that led His people out of slavery.

Too often, Christians seek the hand of God instead of the face of God. Many spotlight the promise of God more than the Promiser. We have been consumed with what God can do *for us* rather than who God is *to us*. The modern day wilderness generation is tired of destructive inclinations, and those who misuse and abuse religion for selfish gain. We desire a true encounter with

God – a real relationship. We would rather suffer in the wilderness with His presence, than stockpile stuff but have no connection to God. We are the generation of minimalists who seek to simplify our lives in hope of finding meaning.

That's why this promise is so special. God will not leave nor forsake you. You are not alone. You may have thousands of Facebook friends or Twitter followers, but still feel alone. You may be so connected to people through work, blogs, and cell phones but are disconnected from reality.

If you feel alone, then you need to know God desires to be intimate with you. His Word says that as you draw near to Him, He will draw near to you. (James 4:8) We have to stop speaking to God like He is way up in the sky somewhere and our prayers take days to reach Him. He is all around us, and if you have accepted Christ, He is in you. He is speaking through every little detail of your life.

Every day around 8:00 in the evening, my wife and I have a special time together. By then, I have returned from work, we have eaten dinner, and put our kids to bed. We have a moment to talk about our day. This is intentional time for us. It's a time when we put our attention and affection to each other. Essentially, we say, "Right now, nothing in the world matters, except you." Sometimes we can be funny during these talks. Sometimes we are serious as we talk about struggles, and sometimes we are encouraging as we talk about what the Lord is teaching us. Each time is different, but it's always intentional, for my wife is the only person in the world I have this type of relationship with.

God wants to have this same kind of relationship with us. If we feel all alone, it's because we haven't made time for Him. We have to set aside a certain time and a certain place to meet with God. Jesus withdrew from His disciples often to spend time with God. If you can't hear God, it's because you have not turned down the noise of life.

> **IF WE FEEL ALL ALONE, IT'S BECAUSE WE HAVEN'T MADE TIME FOR HIM.**

Sometimes I really envy earlier generations because they didn't have the temptation of cell phones. Have you ever wondered how much more of life you would enjoy if you didn't have a cell phone? You could be fully present wherever you are. Until you are fully present, you will not enjoy your relationship with God to the fullest. Set aside a certain time and a certain place just to be with Him.

David said in Psalm 16 that in God's presence, there is fullness of joy. When we are full of something, we are empty of everything else. When we are with God, we are empty of the world, its stress, and pressures. Joshua had the most pressured job of his time. During a grueling 40-year journey, he led 2.5 million people to the Promised Land; a destination concealed for what undoubtedly seemed like an eternity. How did he accomplish this great feat? He knew he was not alone, and he experienced the fullness of joy in God's presence.

"Joy is the infallible sign of the presence of God" - Pierre Teilhard de Chardin

When God is with us, the journey is worthwhile. I enjoy road trips, not because I like being cramped in the car or that I love food at truck stops. I enjoy them because of the memories. Some of my fondest memories of my life with my family or friends were of a road trip. You really get to know people after you have spent a minimum of ten hours in the car with them. God wants to be the driver on our road trip and let us just sit back and enjoy making memories with Him.

One of my favorite Bible stories is about Shadrach, Meshach, and Abednego. These three Hebrew men were thrown into a fiery pit because they would not bow to the king. They knew there was only one true God who deserved this type of worship. The moment they were thrown into the pit, those around them saw a fourth figure in the flame, and realized they were not being burned.

See, when you're in God's presence, you become immune to the attacks of the enemy. "And the light shines in the darkness, and the darkness did not comprehend it." (James 1:5) Light and darkness cannot co-exist. Another root of loneliness occurs when we try to hide things from God. When we try to hide from God, we only deceive ourselves. When do we hide? When we are ashamed.

There is a difference between guilt and shame. Guilt is what we feel when we know we have messed up, but shame says we are the mess up. Don't let shame keep you from God's presence. God convicts us of sin so we can be in right relationship with Him, not so He can rub it in our face.

The presence of God must become normal in our lives, but it also must be revered. In Joshua 5, "The Commander of the Lord's army" appeared to Joshua and instructed him to take off his sandals, for he was standing on holy ground. Removing sandals was a sign of respect and humility. This is how we must view God's presence. We don't deserve it, we can't earn it, and we are not due anything, yet He chooses to dwell among us.

WE MUST NOT FORGET THE PRICE JESUS PAID FOR OUR KINSHIP WITH GOD.

We must not forget the price Jesus paid for our kinship with God. Don't take God's presence for granted, because it came with a cost. In fact, we are instructed to enter God's presence with a specific attitude, thankfulness, and praise. (Psalms 100:4) We should wake up every day with a thankful heart.

If you want to fight entitlement in your life, then take on the challenge to have an attitude of gratitude. **You can't be entitled and thankful at the same time.** We deserve nothing, yet we have been given everything. Our God is worthy of our attention and our praise. God is attracted to our praise. Don't limit praise and worship to a type of music or something you do at church. Praise and worship are a lifestyle to be lived, not a song to sing.

"It is only with gratitude that life becomes rich!"
–Dietrich Bonhoeffer

Every great leader in the Bible, and I dare to say who lived on this earth, has faced loneliness. It's a sign that God is calling you out to a higher level. Jesus said to His disciples, "I no longer call you servants but I call you friends because a servant does not know what his Master is doing." (John 15:15) Jesus was saying to them – we are in this together. Then in the very next chapter, John 17:7, He tells them it is better for Him to leave because a Helper will come.

That Helper is the Holy Spirit. God is up in Heaven, Jesus is at His right hand, and they sent the Holy Spirit to this earth to help us. It has been through the power and presence of the Holy Spirit that I have been able to write this book and live my life. When we invite Jesus into our hearts, the Holy Spirit resides in us. In Acts 1:8 we understand the Holy Spirit can also come upon us to be a witness to the whole earth. Another way to put this is the Holy Spirit will come upon you so that you can reach the promised land God has for you.

The Spirit of God is in us when we get saved, but we have to ask Him to come upon us to receive the boldness to fulfill our mission. If you want to do that today, it's really simple. Just ask for it. Say, "Holy Spirit, come upon me, just like You did with the disciples in Acts 2:4, that I will have the power of God to fulfill the mission You have given me." When you pray this prayer, be open to feel and hear the voice of the Holy Spirit. For further understanding and theology about the Holy Spirit, read a great book by Robert Morris entitled, *The God I Never Knew*.

Pastor's Challenge:

My prayer for you is that you would spend time seeking God whenever you feel alone. Remember, if you receive the promise, but miss Him, then you have failed. Don't be so busy chasing a dream or a purpose that you forget the One who called you. He is the One who started this journey and He wants you to succeed just as much as you do. All throughout the Bible, men and women weathered a wilderness experience. The wilderness experience is designed to bring you closer to God so you can see the character of God and then be more like Him. If you find God in the wilderness, then you will celebrate with Him in the promise. Whether you're a man or woman, I'm praying you will see yourself as a Joshua who God has called to lead His people out of the wilderness and into the promise.

Continue to ask God what the role of the Holy Spirit is in your life. Churches have done weird things in the name of the Holy Spirit, but the Holy Spirit is not weird. The Holy Spirit is practical and personal.

CONCLUSION

"Being confident of this very thing, that He who has begun a good work in you will complete it until the day of Jesus Christ" (Philippians 1:6 NKJV)

Well, dear reader, you made it to the end! You may be asking, "So why have a conclusion?" It's because I want to speak to you on a personal level. As I was writing this I was asking the Lord, "Who will be reading this book?" And with that thought in mind, I believe there are five groups of people who are reading this right now. My hope is that you will relate to one of these groups and I will be able to encourage you in who God has called you to be, and where God is calling you to go.

I love the opening verse of this chapter because we are commanded to be confident that GOD will complete what He started. The pressure is on Him, not on any of us. All of us who believe in Christ, come to Him by way of a miracle. When we first started our journey in relationship with Jesus, we were overwhelmed with gratitude and awe. But somewhere along the line, we started thinking it was up to us to complete this journey God started. The truth is – the dream God has given you was first His dream for you, and, it is our job to give it back to Him. It is important for us to put it back into His hands and to be confident He will complete this work.

The Newcomer

The first group I want to talk to is what I call the "Newcomer." If you haven't spent your whole life in church and you are new to the whole idea of a relationship with Jesus, you are a newcomer. Perhaps as you read through this book, there were many foreign concepts and principles you are still mulling over. Maybe you are just starting to understand and fathom the love God has for you and how

He displayed it by sending His Son, Jesus. You are in an amazing place in life! This is just the beginning.

Throughout the book I have used Joshua as a great example of how God can take an impossible situation and a group of wandering people, to reach a God-ordained promised land. Something we must all remember is that Joshua was a picture of Christ. He gave us a prophetic vision of Jesus, who was to come. There are a few indicators that let us make this assumption. First, the names Joshua and Jesus mean the same thing. Then there's Joshua's character and his style of leadership. In many of the leaders of the Old Testament, we see "types" or pictures of Christ that point prophetically to what is to come. That is why we read the Bible as many books that make up one seamless story and not many books that lead in different directions and storylines. As we learn about who Joshua was, we are, in large measure, learning about who Jesus is now. Jesus is our ultimate example. Our goal is that we will love as He loved, live as He lived, and dwell where He dwells. When we live like Jesus, we know there will be great rewards for us in eternity. As a Christ follower, our focus is on eternity and Heaven. How we live on earth will determine how we spend eternity.

AS A CHRIST FOLLOWER OUR FOCUS IS ON ETERNITY AND HEAVEN.

If you are a newcomer, I first challenge you to find a local church that believes in the centrality of Jesus Christ. Second, I challenge you to take inventory of your surroundings. For you to reach the promised land, you might have to cut off some of your relationships, stop going to some of the places where you have always gone, and some of you might even need to choose a new job or career path. "Do not be deceived, bad company corrupts good character." (1 Corinthians 15:33.) Third, I would challenge you to study the life of Jesus. Jesus is the goal, He is the model, and He is the center of our faith. You will never be more in the will of God than when you are endeavoring to be like Him.

The Doubters

The second group I want to speak to are those who I call the Doubters. If you have grown up in church, heard endless sermons, perhaps prayed thousands of times, yet you doubt the relevance of Christianity, then you fall into this group. I hope you caught that the essence of this book was not to get you to come back to church, but rather, that you become who God called you to be and then realize the importance of the church. It is never bad to question the beliefs you were brought up with. How else are you going to make those principles your own beliefs? I remember in school, and sometimes in church, when a teacher or pastor would say, "Hold questions for the end." But it always seemed like there was never really time for questions. So, we grew up never understanding the importance of asking questions or more importantly, asking the right questions.

Just think for a moment about the generation born in the wilderness under Moses. The Bible called the parents, stiff-necked, whiners, and stubborn. What a great spiritual climate the Joshua generation grew up in! First of all, they had no home. Second, they had to eat the same thing every day and they walked around in circles in a desert for 40 years. On top of that, their parents were whining and complaining all the time about this "God" that freed them from bondage. That new generation might have had a reason to deny their faith, perhaps even settle in the wilderness and say there was no promised land.

Well, you are faced with that same choice today. You can deny the existence of God, or His relevance, and decide to settle in the wilderness. Truth be told, I have seen many do this and they live unfulfilled, unhappy lives because deep down inside, they know they were meant for something so much greater.

So, if you want to move from being a doubter to a Joshua, your first steps should be to ask the right questions. You need to start seeking God with these three questions. Number one, "God, what is my purpose on earth?" Number two, "God, will You please speak to me through Your Word?" Number three, "God, will You confirm the call on my life?" I truly believe if you ask God those three questions and pursue the answers you get, you will hear and know how God wants you to walk into your own promised land. God wants to hear the inquiries of your heart. He wants to answer your deepest fears and disputes. Don't let hurt feelings, bad leadership, and failure stop you from getting back in the game.

> **HE WANTS TO ANSWER YOUR DEEPEST FEARS AND DISPUTES.**

In the Middle

The third group I want to talk to is what I call those who are in the Middle. You are in the middle of pursuing your promise. You have taken God at His word, you have taken leaps of faith, and you are waiting to see where it will lead you. You are a modern day Joshua. You have accepted the call and you are pursuing the promise. I want you to believe me when I tell you, "You will always be the most tempted to give up when you are closest to your miracle."

I don't know how Joshua dealt with his emotions (and perhaps pride) when he had to wander in the wilderness for 40 years because no one around him could see the potential he saw in the Promised Land. Oh, man! I'm sure he had to hold his tongue so many times. You see, when you are in the "middle", people don't understand you. They might even question your sanity. They start to wonder if perhaps you missed it this time, but you know deep down in your heart you are pursuing the promised land. "Therefore do not cast away your confidence, which has great reward. For you have need of endurance, so that after you have done the will of God, you may receive the promise:" (Hebrews 10:35-36) Don't let the opinions of others or the naysayers sway your confidence. Your confidence will produce a great reward. Keep going, keep pushing, keep believing. Don't stop!

Some of you in the middle have started businesses, you have chosen career paths, or even moved to a new location. Perhaps you stepped out in faith and you have begun to dream the impossible. I think what got Joshua through the middle is that he held onto the promise of God. What's your promise? What has God spoken to you? Don't forget it. Write it down, put it on your bathroom mirror, speak it and pray over it. Don't let setbacks destroy your zeal. There is a process I see when Joshua stepped out. **People first called him a nobody, then they called him crazy, and they called him for advice.**

The Settlers

The fourth group is what I call the Settlers. A settler is somebody who occupies and develops a place where there has been no inhabitants. If you are a settler, then you have taken the Joshua mandate on your life. You have faced many trials, won many battles, and you are in the promised land. The promised land is a place of influence God has given you where nobody else has been before. If that's you, then praise God for your faithfulness, for your commitment, and for your dedication to the cause of Christ.

I have met a few young leaders who are in this position. God has given them miraculous opportunities to change the world at an early age. Joshua's main job once he reached the Promised Land was to divide and distribute the land among the 12 tribes. But it was not for them alone. It was also for the generations after them. I challenge you; if you are living in the promised land of God, begin to share your success, disciple leaders, and build for the next generation. Each generation after us will have to make a choice, just like we are making – as to whether they will follow God. Let us leave the legacy of a promise fulfilled---

not delayed. Let us leave a legacy of humble obedience, not stiff-necked stubbornness. Let us leave a legacy of culture shifters. Let us empower the next generation.

LET US LEAVE A LEGACY OF HUMBLE OBEDIENCE NOT STIFF-NECKED STUBBORNNESS.

Moses

The fifth and final group which might be the most important of all, are the Moses group. Moses believed in Joshua, he prepared Joshua, and he set him up for success. Moses was not a perfect leader, but he was a godly leader. If you desire to see millennials reach their full potential and you want to see the lineage of faith continue in this generation, then you are a Moses.

I don't believe a generation has to die, like Moses' generation did, before Joshuas are elevated. If Moses and the children of Israel had believed in Joshua and Caleb, then Israel would never have had to remain in the wilderness. I plead with you as a millennial – believe in the next generation. Don't lose hope. We are worth fighting for. Though the culture may look more and more godless, there are many out there who see an opportunity to let the Light shine through us. We need mentors, fathers, mothers, and leaders in our lives.

I believe the world's greatest wisdom is within you and we need it. You have life experience. You have great stories of faith. You have seen the goodness of God and we need you. If you are a Moses, then find a Joshua, and look for somebody to pour your life into. The model of discipleship in the Bible is that the mentee is chosen by the mentor. Don't wait for somebody to come knocking on your door, go look for them. Look for opportunities to share your life with others. Jesus chose the 12 disciples, Elijah chose Elisha, and Moses chose Joshua. In your business today, in your family today, in your church today, there are young millennials looking for somebody to believe in them. To say, "God has a promised land for you and I want to help you reach it." I believe we will see God move like never before when generations begin to unify under one common goal – to see God glorified on this earth.

To contact or share your thoughts with the Author visit:

www.LanceAinsworth.com

www.Facebook.com/Lance.Ainsworth

www.Twitter.com/LanceAinsworth

www.Instagram.com/Lance_Ainsworth

email: PastorLAinsworth@gmail.com

Made in the USA
San Bernardino, CA
05 December 2017